WHEN EVERYTHING WENT WRONG

10 Real Stories of Inventors Who Didn't Give Up!

ILLUSTRATIONS BY AGNESE INNOCENTE

TEXT BY MAX TEMPORELLI AND BARBARA GOZZI

Andrews McMeel
PUBLISHING®

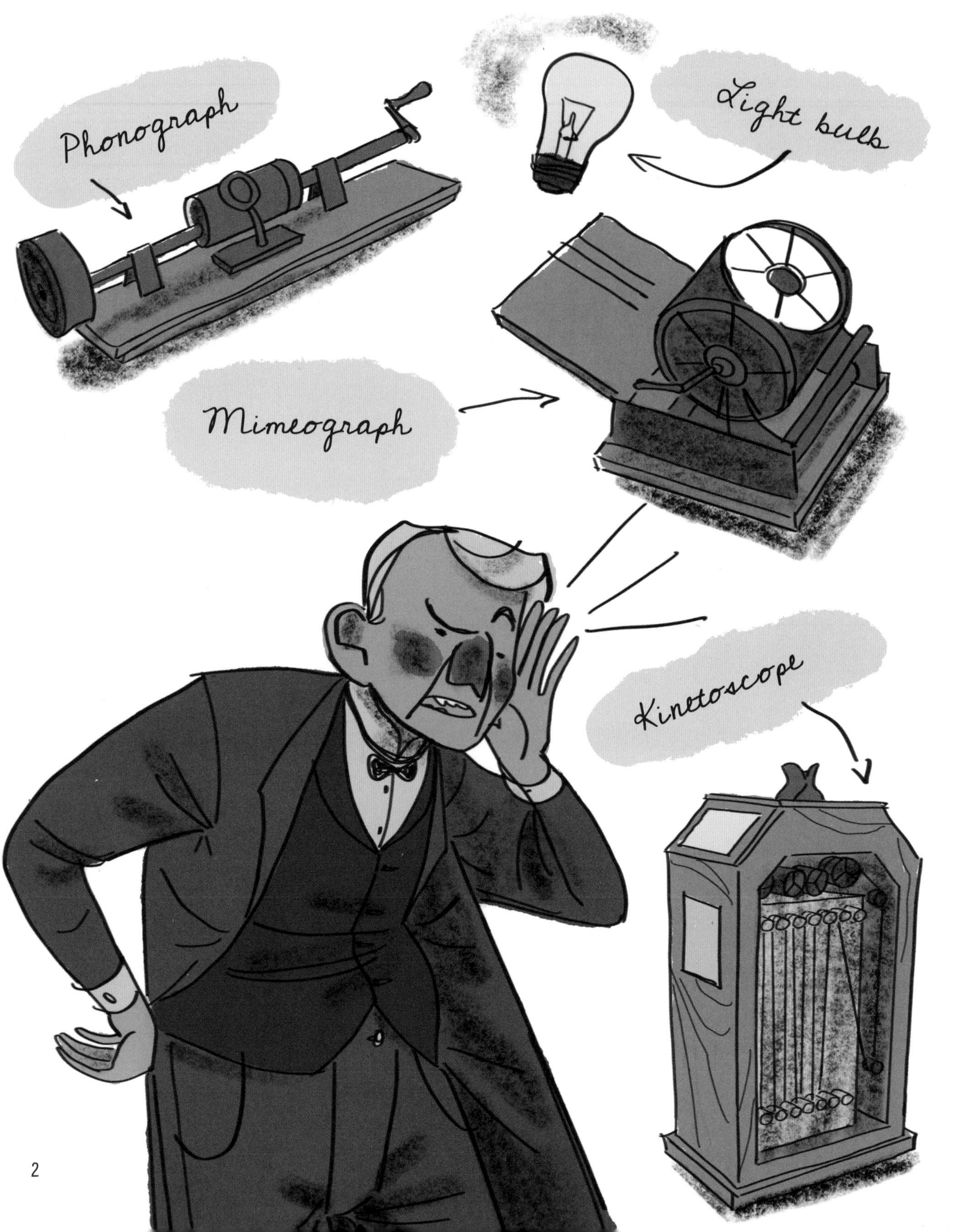
Phonograph
Light bulb
Mimeograph
Kinetoscope

Thomas Alva Edison

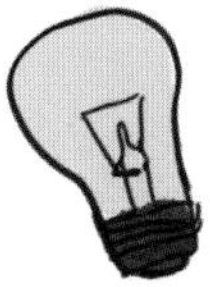

Thomas Alva Edison was very curious and a highly accomplished inventor. But did you know that inventing the light bulb was very hard for him?

Thomas Edison was born on February 11, 1847, in Milan, Ohio. His ears did not function well, and due to his partial deafness, he would struggle to follow lessons in class. He couldn't hear many low sounds, like the noise made by his six brothers! So his mother taught him at home, and Thomas learned to concentrate. At age 11, he had his own chemistry laboratory in the Edisons' cellar.

One day he saw a child playing beside the train tracks and grabbed him before a train passed. The child was saved! The child's father was the stationmaster, and as a way to thank Thomas, he taught him how to use the telegraph, which was an early version of a phone. Thomas immediately fell in love with it! At 17, he improved upon how the telegraph sent messages, and at 29, he had laboratories built in New Jersey, where he started new tests and inventions with his assistants.

Thomas loved to constantly explore and design, even if, sometimes, years would pass before an invention worked! Among his many ideas, he invented the phonograph (the first device to record and reproduce sounds), the mimeograph (an ancestor of the printer), and the kinetoscope (a precursor to the film projector). However, inventing the light bulb proved tricky . . . and Thomas almost couldn't do it. His mistakes ended up paving the way to success!

Turn the page to read about how he invented the light bulb . . .
despite it taking a LONG time!

In the NJ laboratory:

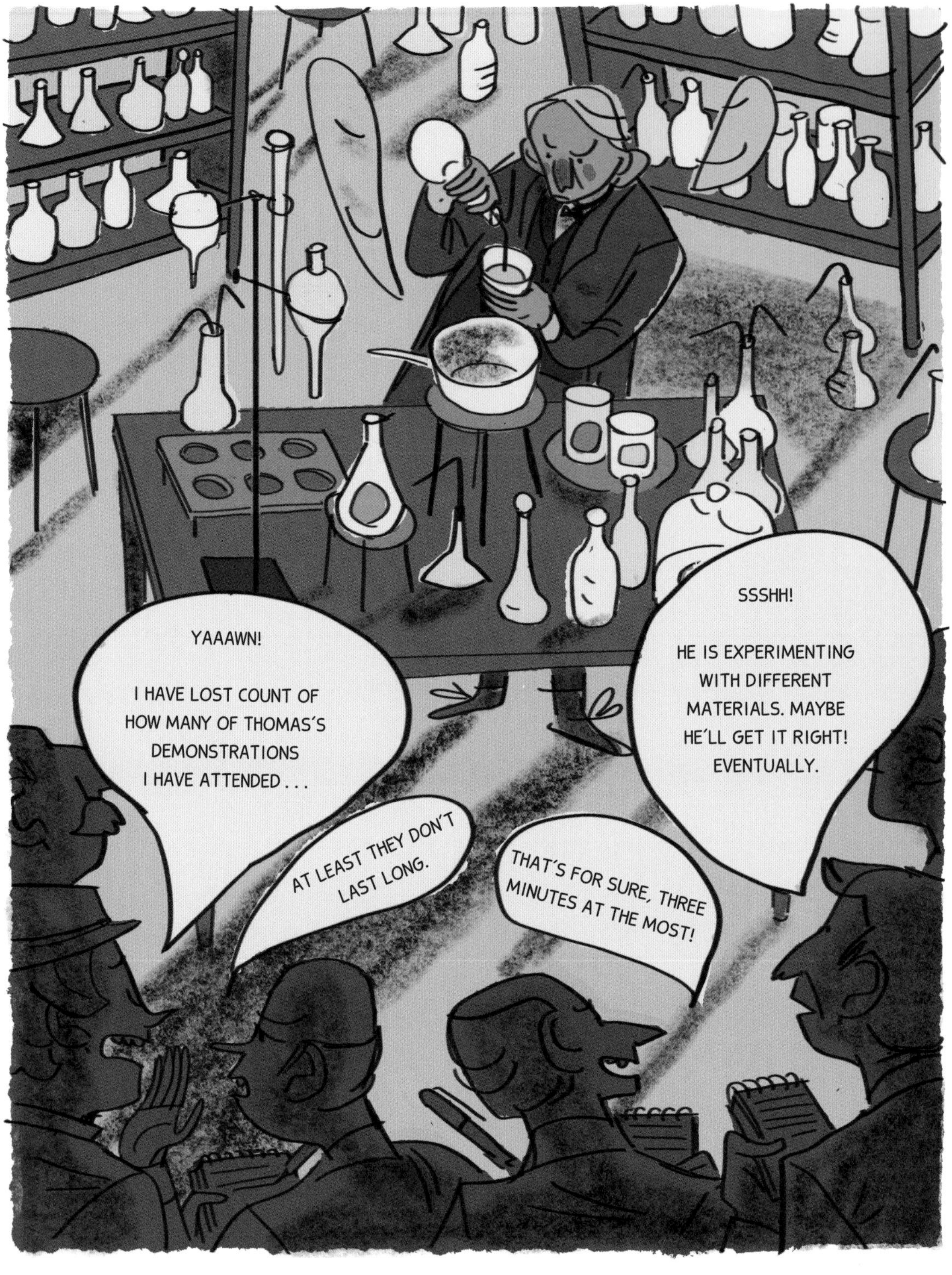
YAAAWN!
I HAVE LOST COUNT OF HOW MANY OF THOMAS'S DEMONSTRATIONS I HAVE ATTENDED . . .
SSSHH!
HE IS EXPERIMENTING WITH DIFFERENT MATERIALS. MAYBE HE'LL GET IT RIGHT! EVENTUALLY.
AT LEAST THEY DON'T LAST LONG.
THAT'S FOR SURE, THREE MINUTES AT THE MOST!

Until one day...

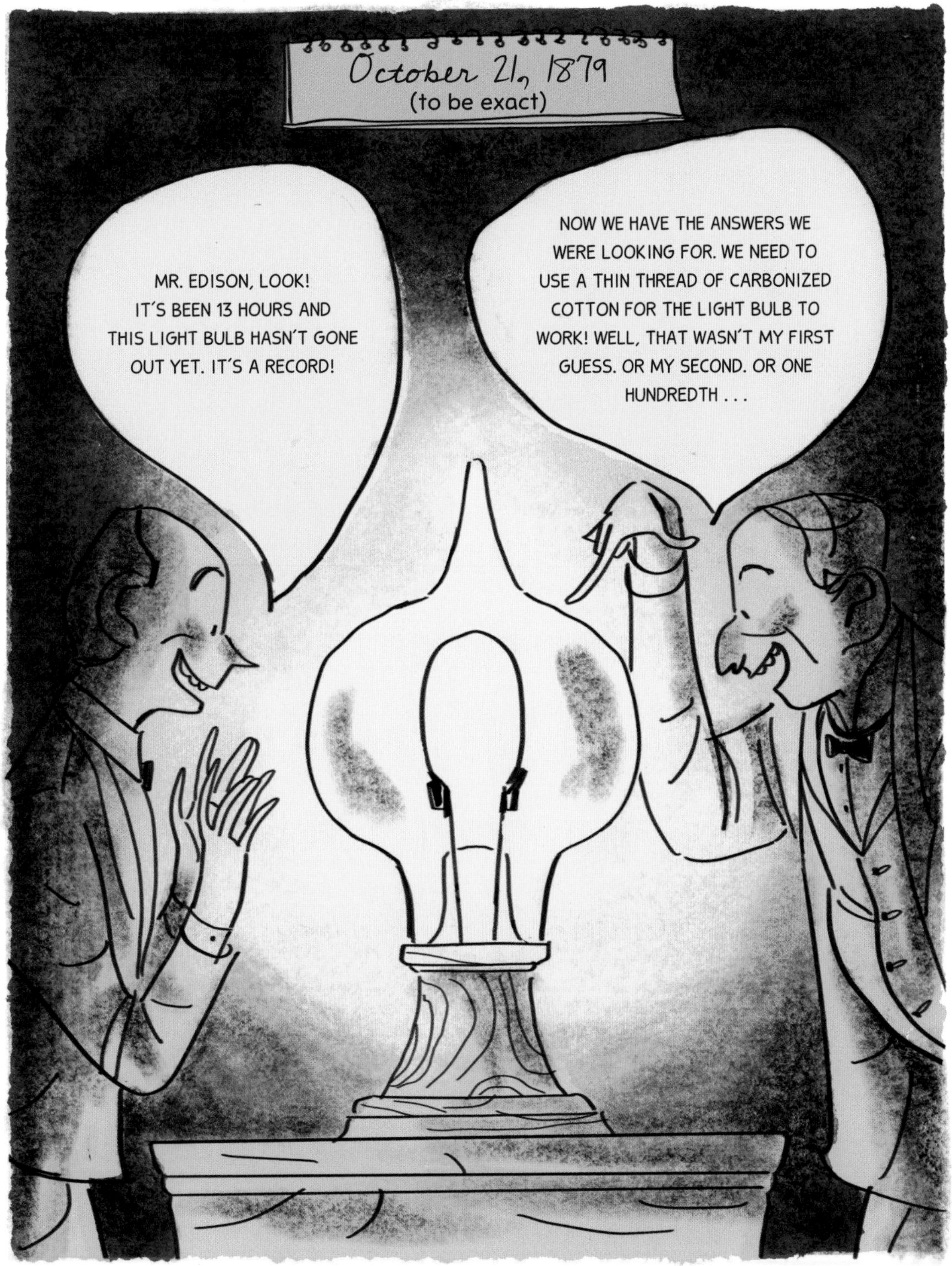
October 21, 1879
(to be exact)
MR. EDISON, LOOK! IT'S BEEN 13 HOURS AND THIS LIGHT BULB HASN'T GONE OUT YET. IT'S A RECORD!
NOW WE HAVE THE ANSWERS WE WERE LOOKING FOR. WE NEED TO USE A THIN THREAD OF CARBONIZED COTTON FOR THE LIGHT BULB TO WORK! WELL, THAT WASN'T MY FIRST GUESS. OR MY SECOND. OR ONE HUNDREDTH . . .

"I have not failed 10,000 times. I have not failed once. I have succeeded in proving that those 10,000 ways will not work. When I have eliminated the ways that will not work, I will find the way that will work."

Thomas Edison

As you can see, Thomas had tried to invent the light bulb many times and failed. Yet all of his attempts were necessary: One less and Edison would not have understood how to do it. But he also learned a lot from the mistakes of others.

For example, in 1878 the English chemist Joseph Swan was the first to build and turn on an incandescent light bulb.

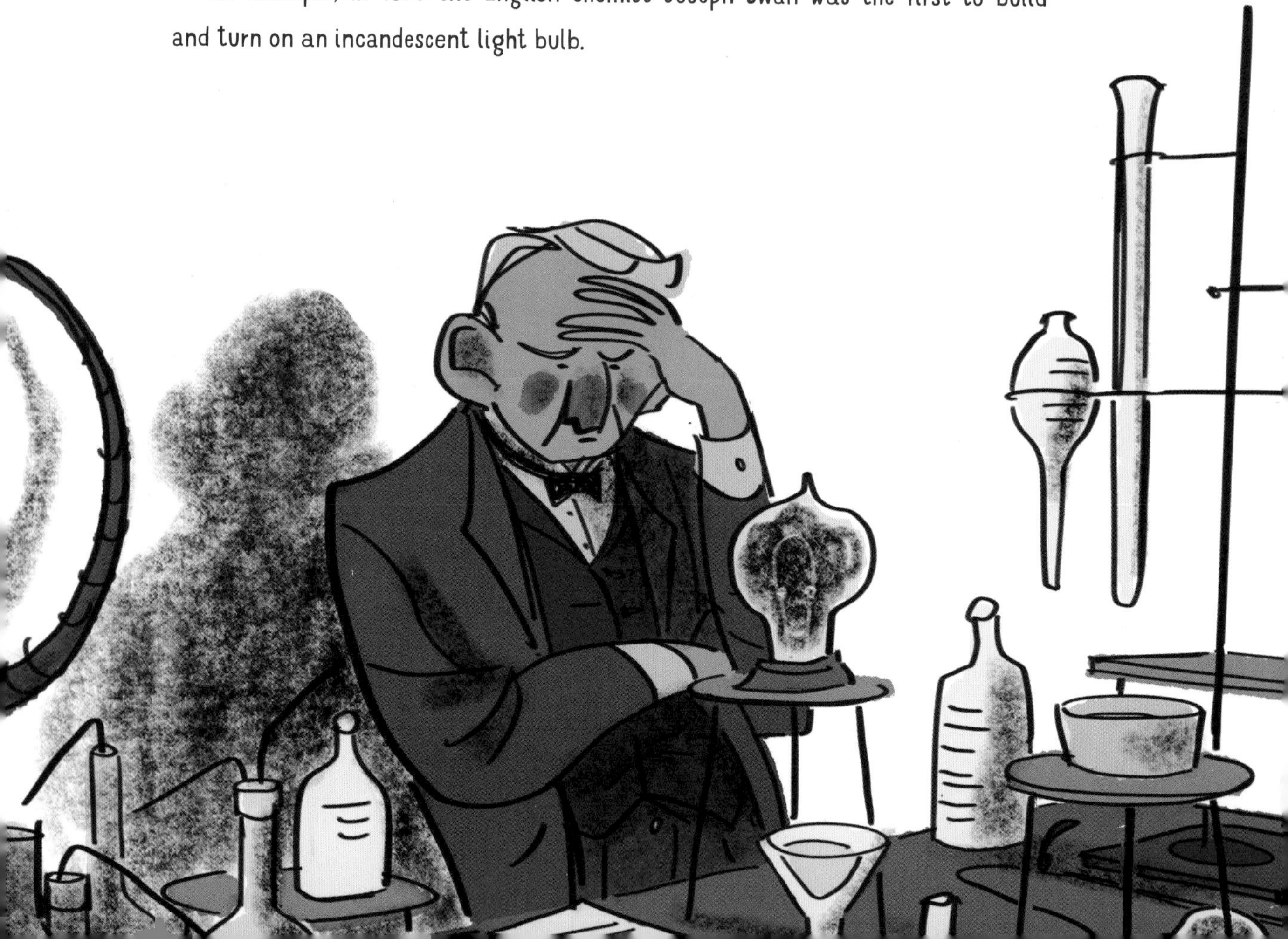

But the light bulb built by Swan had a problem: The incandescent carbon filament emitted so much soot that it quickly covered the inside of the bulb (the glass coating). That's right, everything became black!

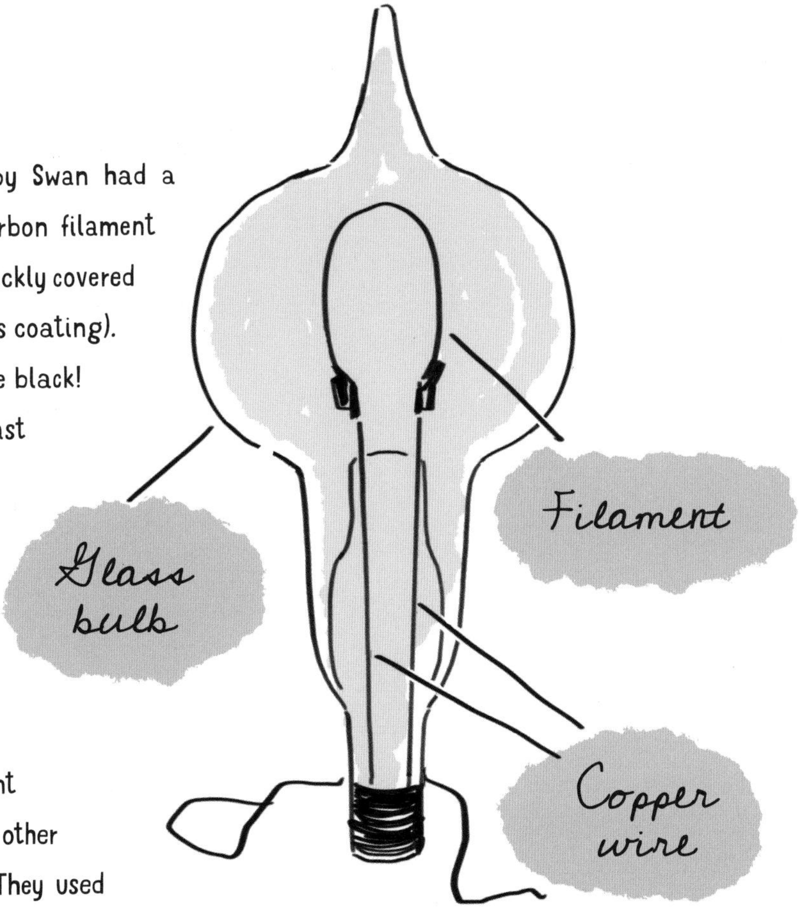
Glass bulb
Filament
Copper wire

In short, the light did not last long, just a few minutes. Plus, the light bulb consumed a lot of electricity. Swan's invention did not work.

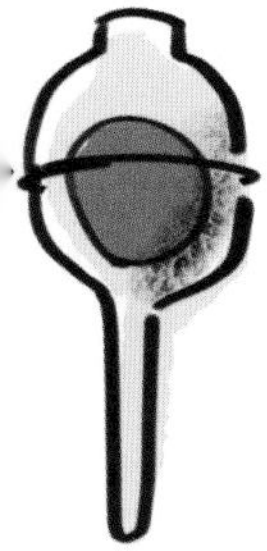

Thomas started with Swan's idea and tried to improve it through many different experiments along with the other researchers in his laboratory. They used filaments from different materials, such as platinum and vegetable fibers. Eventually, something happened with charred cotton: The inside of the bulb didn't become completely black, and the light lasted longer!

On October 21, 1879, for 13 and a half hours, the incandescent light bulb shone. Then he worked for the next few weeks on making it shine even longer. That is how Thomas Alva Edison invented the light bulb: by learning from mistakes!

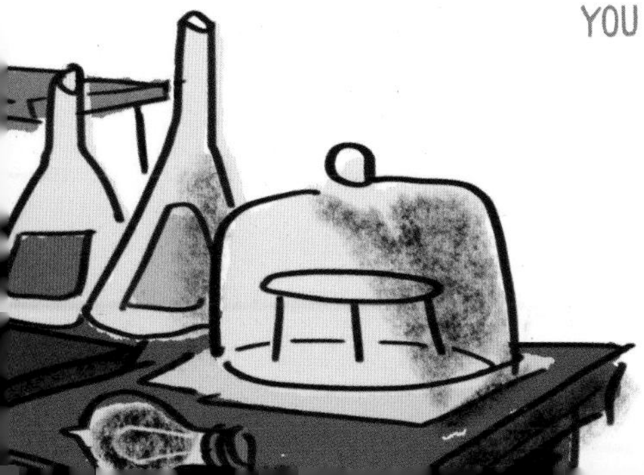

YOU CAN LEARN FROM MISTAKES, AND WHEN YOU BELIEVE IN AN IDEA, YOU MUST NEVER STOP PURSUING IT.

Thomas Alva Edison

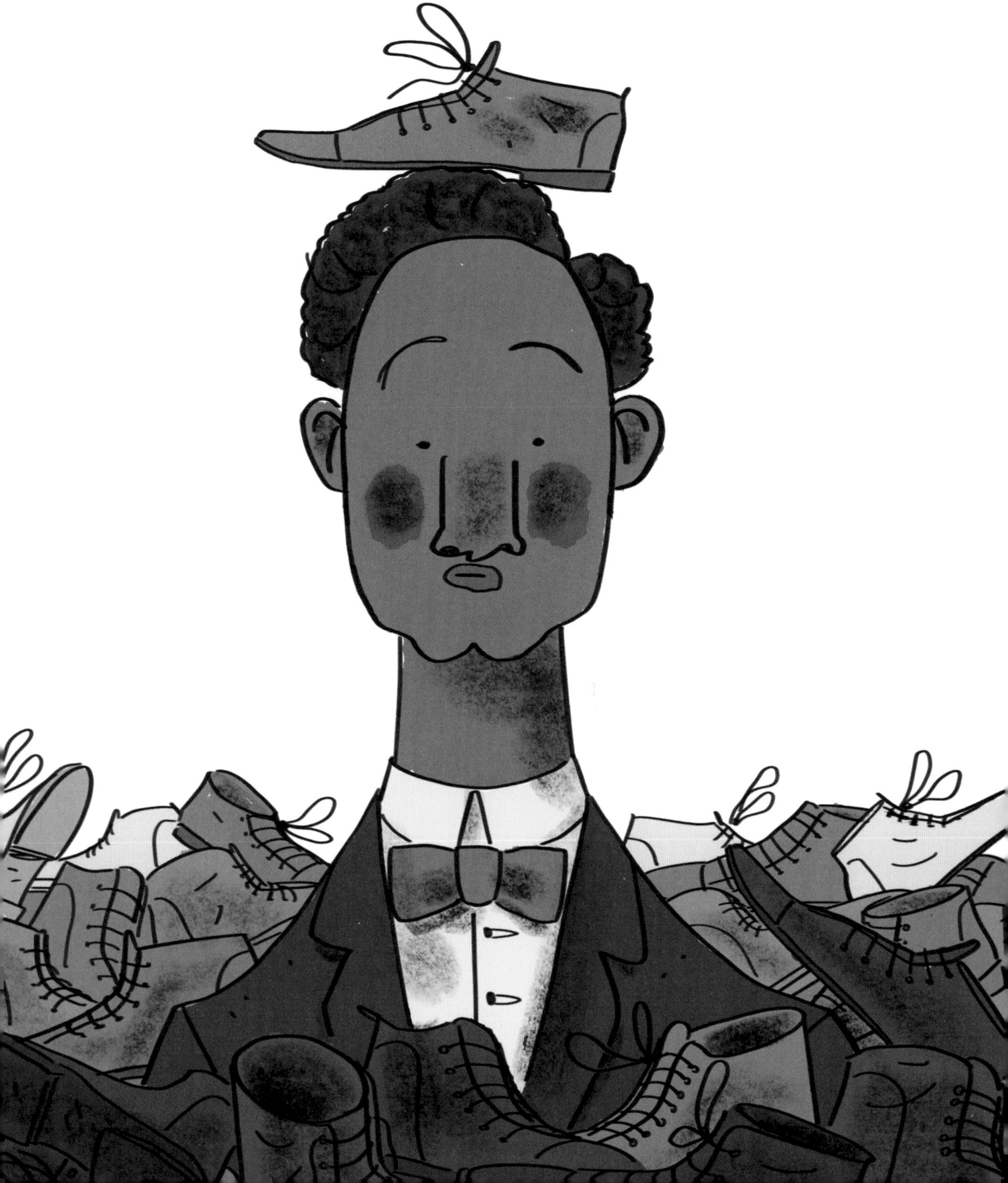

Jan Ernst Matzeliger

**Jan Ernst Matzeliger had a great passion
for mechanics and machinery.**

Jan Ernst Matzeliger was born on September 15, 1852, in what is now the small country of Suriname in South America. His father was an engineer, and it was thanks to him that Jan discovered the "magic" of mechanics. By age 10, he was already helping his father in his workshops. He loved getting his hands dirty! But Jan also wanted to see the world, so when he turned 19, he embarked as a sailor on a merchant ship.

Jan spoke only Dutch when, a few years later, he decided to settle in the United States. He was a loner, but he rolled up his sleeves and learned English. Jan soon found work in a shoe factory in Massachusetts, where he realized that something was less than ideal with the manufacturing process. Some of the leatherworking procedures were still done by hand, which was very time-consuming and also prone to error. He immediately set to work. Jan knew his beloved mechanics could improve the situation, but it wasn't easy for him.

At first, many people didn't believe in Jan's ideas, but he kept trying. Throughout his life he worked on solutions, designing mechanisms and small machinery that helped workers in the footwear industry. And thanks to his commitment, making shoes became easier and less expensive. This way more and more people were able to keep their feet warm and walk better!

Turn the page to learn how he did it!

How it used to be:

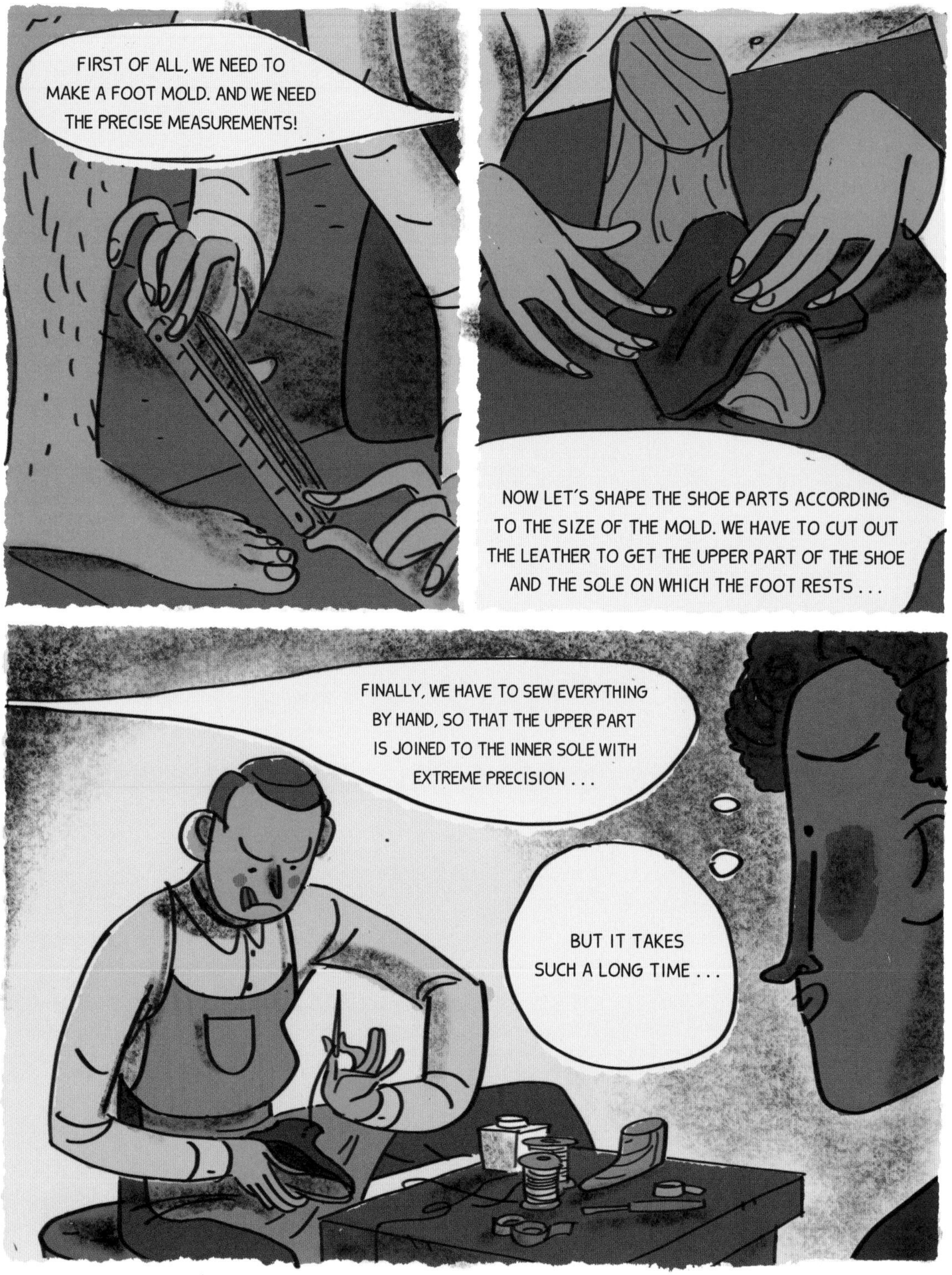
FIRST OF ALL, WE NEED TO MAKE A FOOT MOLD. AND WE NEED THE PRECISE MEASUREMENTS!
NOW LET'S SHAPE THE SHOE PARTS ACCORDING TO THE SIZE OF THE MOLD. WE HAVE TO CUT OUT THE LEATHER TO GET THE UPPER PART OF THE SHOE AND THE SOLE ON WHICH THE FOOT RESTS . . .
FINALLY, WE HAVE TO SEW EVERYTHING BY HAND, SO THAT THE UPPER PART IS JOINED TO THE INNER SOLE WITH EXTREME PRECISION . . .
BUT IT TAKES SUCH A LONG TIME . . .

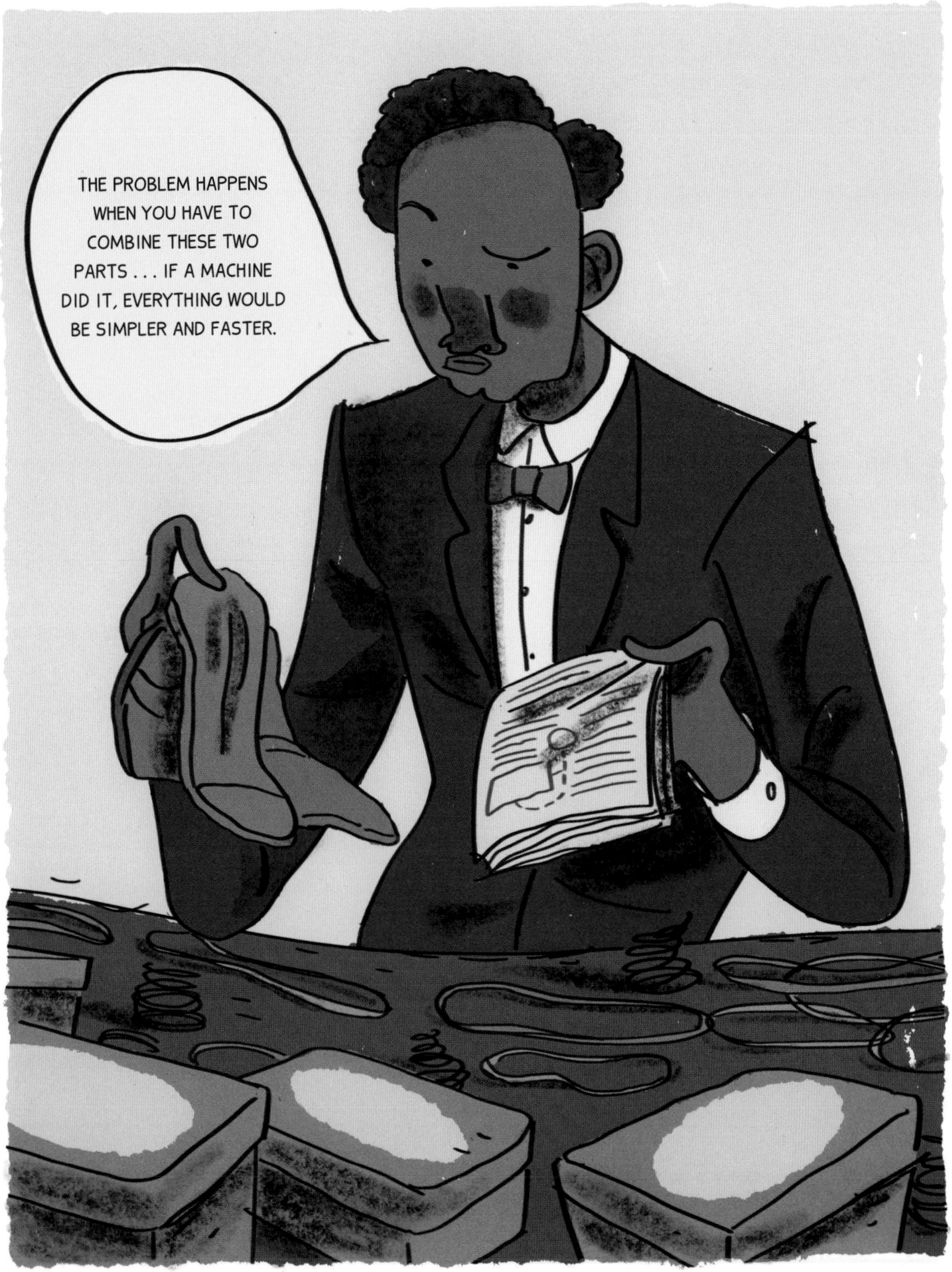
THE PROBLEM HAPPENS WHEN YOU HAVE TO COMBINE THESE TWO PARTS . . . IF A MACHINE DID IT, EVERYTHING WOULD BE SIMPLER AND FASTER.

Matzeliger only needed to observe the production of the shoes to understand that there was a problem. But solving it wasn't easy! However, he was sure he could find a solution.

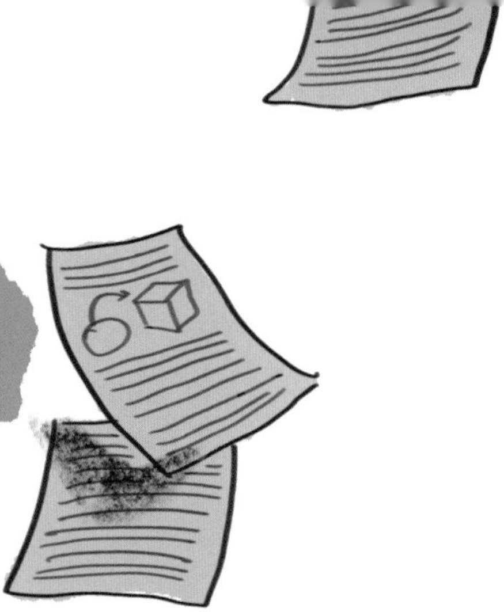

He conceived a device that attached the upper part of the shoe to the sole . . . all automatically! Unlike human hands, the machine was faster and more accurate. He explained it in detail in a document (15 thickly written pages), but no one understood anything about it! He then made models to show how his invention worked.

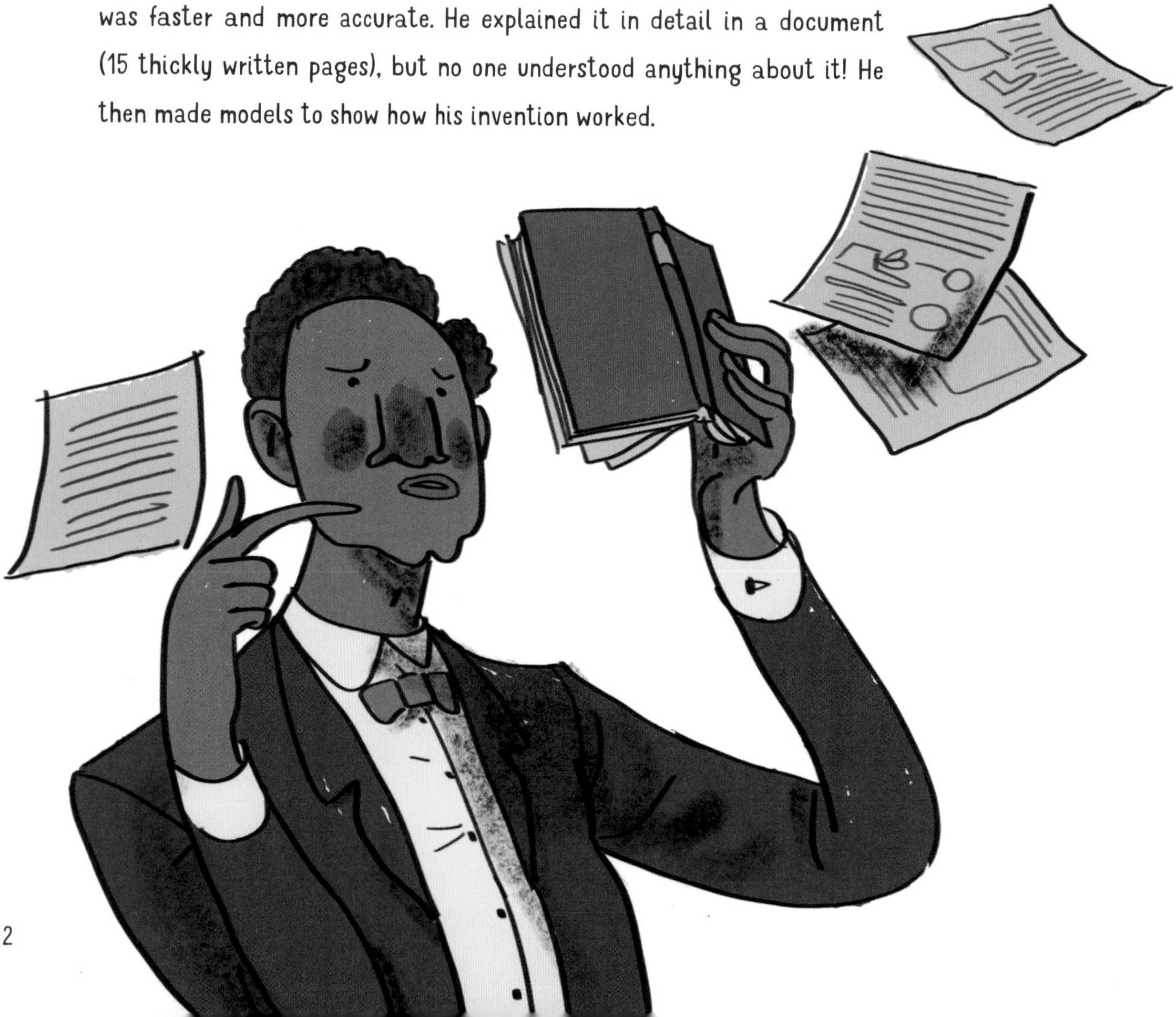

Unfortunately, the other shoemakers would stare at the moving machinery, shaking their heads. Many had tried before, but in the end, no machine could replace human hands . . . plus all those mechanical devices were really complicated!

"Maybe I'm wrong," thought Matzeliger, perplexed. "My invention could be a mistake."

But he continued to try, studying every book he found.

Then, in 1883, his last prototype succeeded in completing every step in a clear and precise way. How? The machine would hold the shoe steady while pulling the leather around the heel, then it would fasten the insole with nails. At this point, the cycle would finish and the completed shoe would be pushed out into a container. Only the final finishing touches were missing (such as inserting the laces).

In one day, Matzeliger's invention could produce 10 times the number of shoes that people by hand could normally make. Talk about a great invention!

WHAT APPEARS TO BE A MISTAKE
MAY JUST BE SOMETHING NEW
TO UNDERSTAND.

Jan Ernst Matzeliger

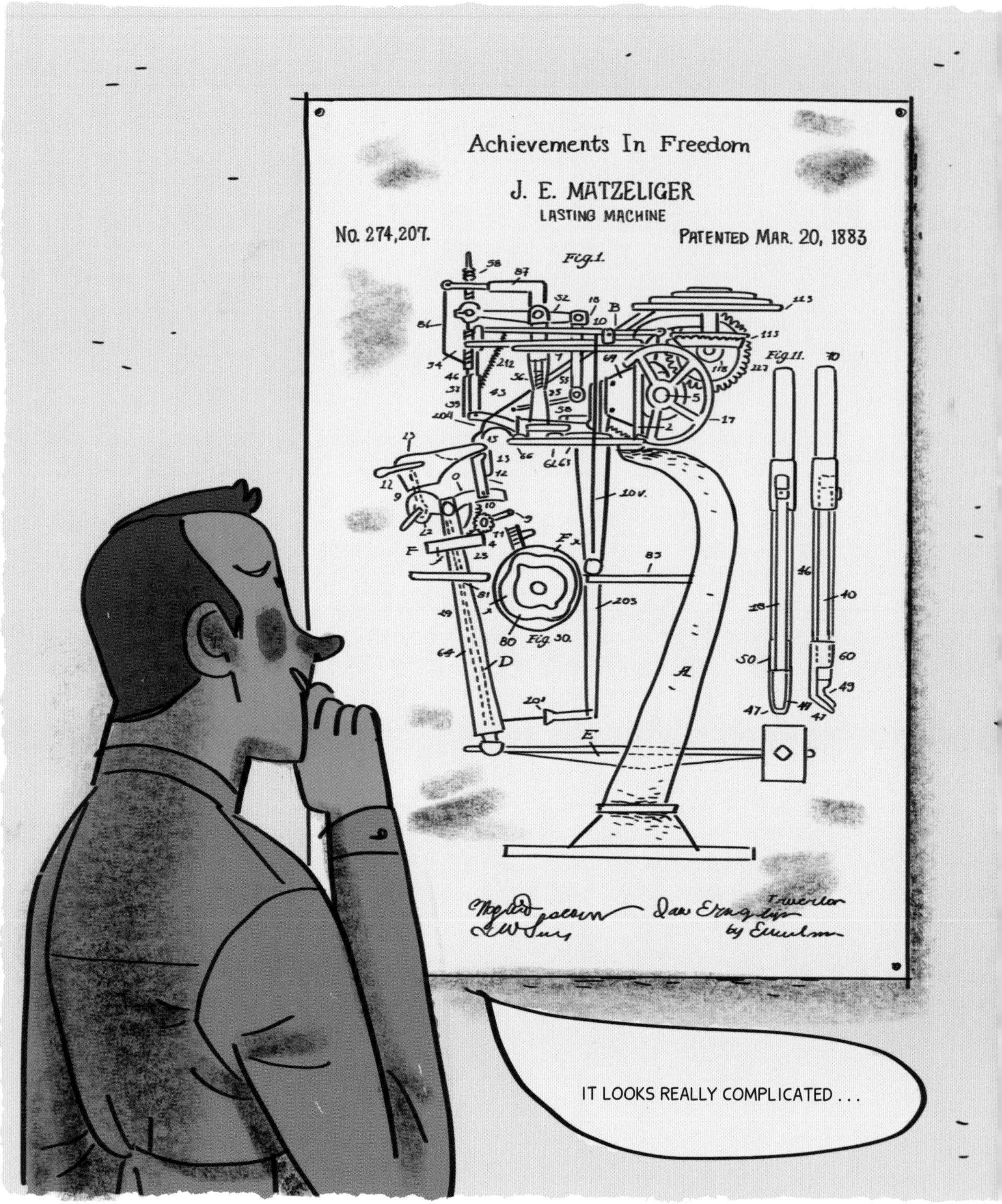
Achievements In Freedom
J. E. MATZELIGER
LASTING MACHINE
No. 274,207.
PATENTED MAR. 20, 1883
Fig. 1.
Fig. 11.
Fig. 30.
IT LOOKS REALLY COMPLICATED . . .

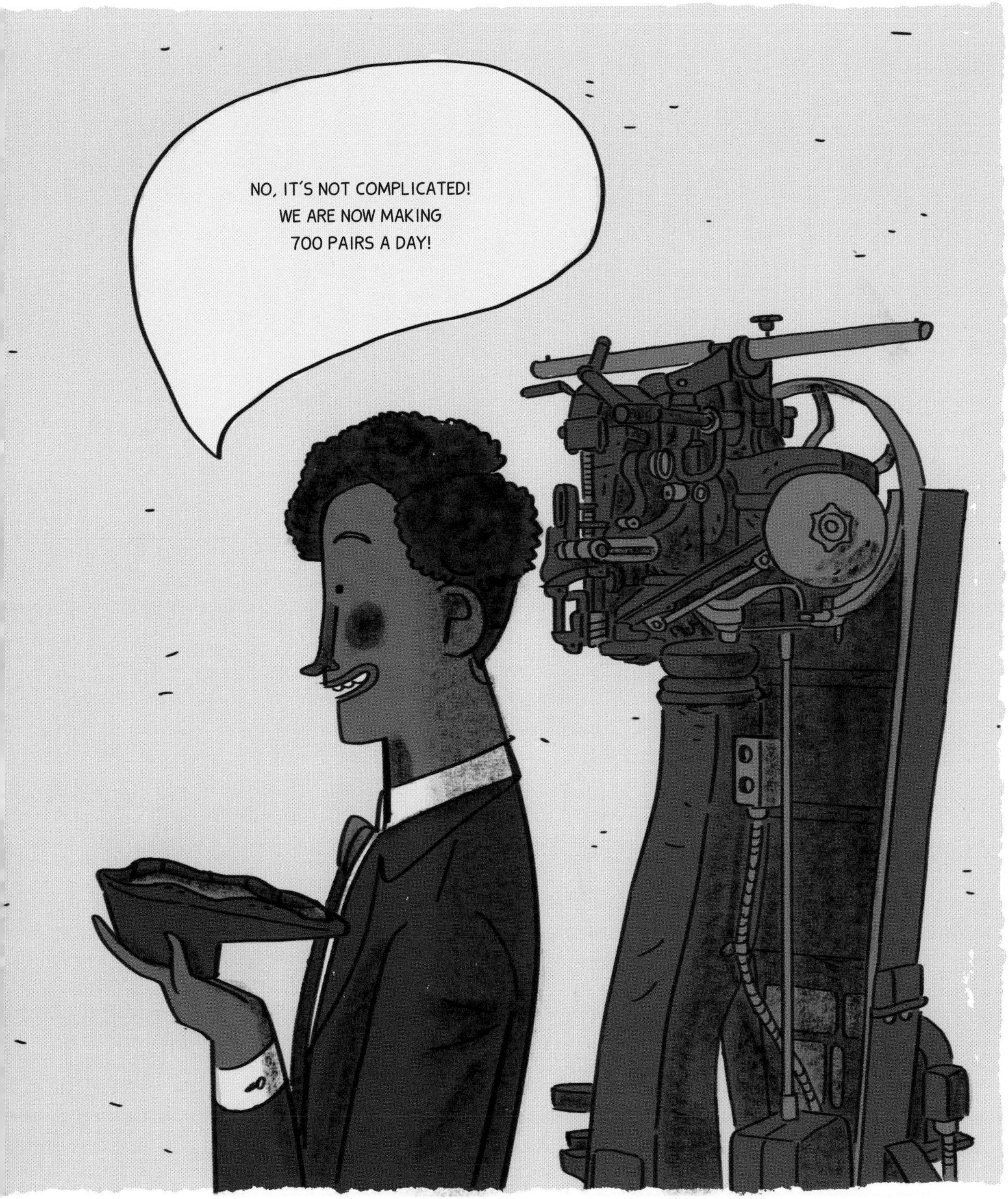
NO, IT'S NOT COMPLICATED! WE ARE NOW MAKING 700 PAIRS A DAY!

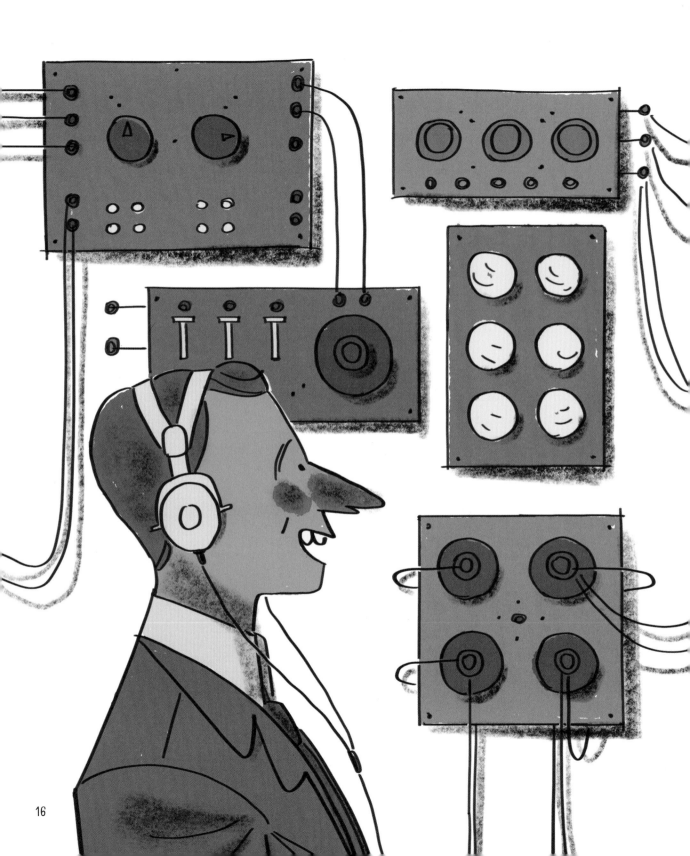

Guglielmo Marconi

**Guglielmo Marconi was fascinated by technologies
that improved everyday life.**

Guglielmo Marconi was born on April 25, 1874, in Bologna, Italy. From an early age, physics laboratories were his second home, so much that, at the age of 18, he set one up in his father's villa.

Among his many interests were radio waves, which were capable of transmitting sounds over a distance. Marconi wanted to discover a way to send signals far away, without cables, unlike the electric telegraph.

In 1896, he moved to England, where he created his first company to develop "wireless telegraphy." He experimented everywhere, including aboard an ocean liner and on a battleship. His discoveries made it possible to improve safety at sea with more effective and timely maritime radio services.

In 1909, after developing wireless telegraphy over 15 years, he won the Nobel Prize in Physics, along with German scientist Karl Ferdinand Braun. But Marconi continued to experiment. In 1930 he established a connection between the equipment on a ship in the port of Genoa and a radio station in Australia. The radio signal traveled nearly 10,500 miles, turning on the lights in Sydney City Hall!

How did he do it? Well, you're about to find out!

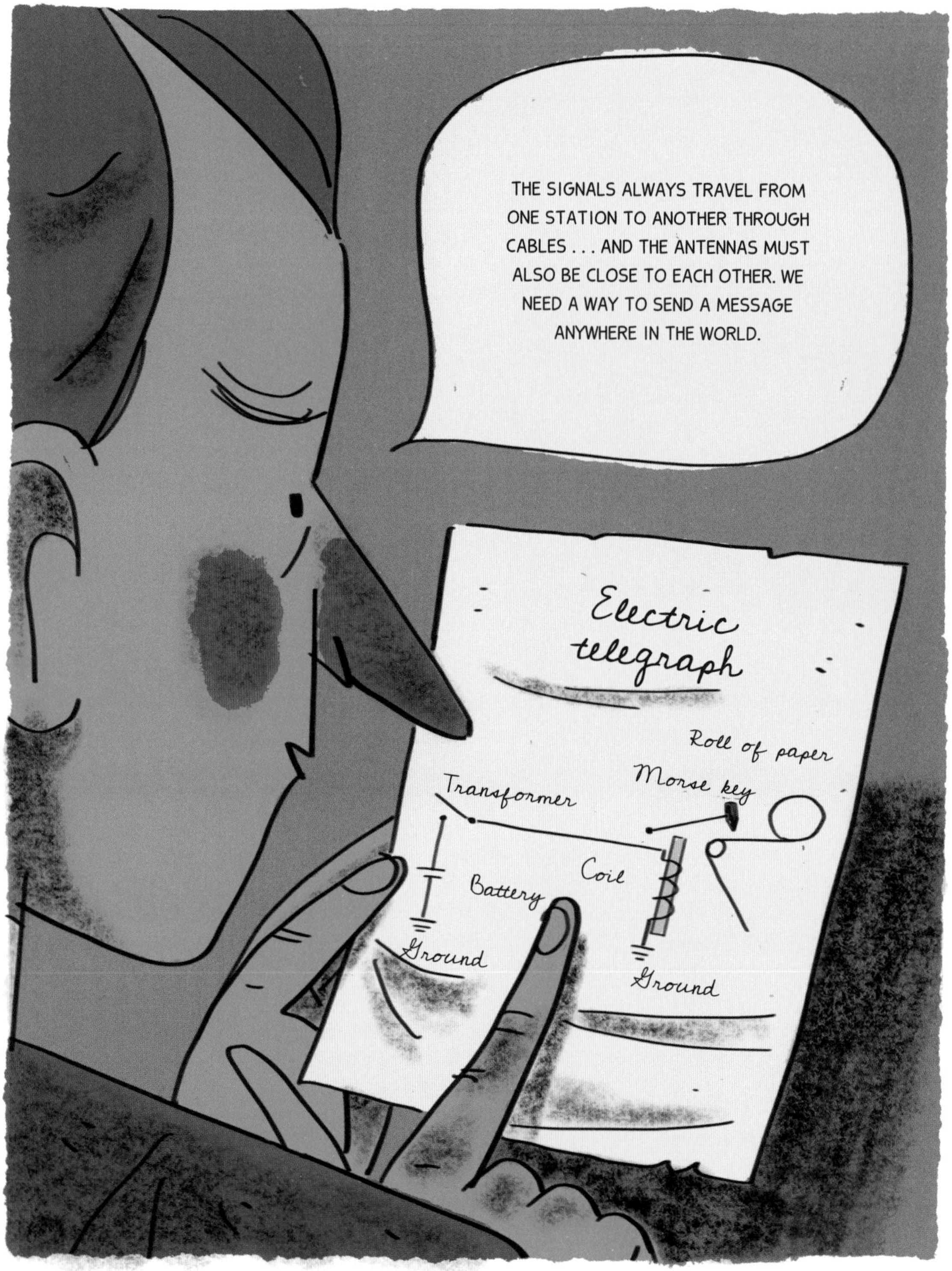
THE SIGNALS ALWAYS TRAVEL FROM ONE STATION TO ANOTHER THROUGH CABLES . . . AND THE ANTENNAS MUST ALSO BE CLOSE TO EACH OTHER. WE NEED A WAY TO SEND A MESSAGE ANYWHERE IN THE WORLD.
Electric telegraph
Roll of paper
Morse key
Transformer
Coil
Battery
Ground
Ground

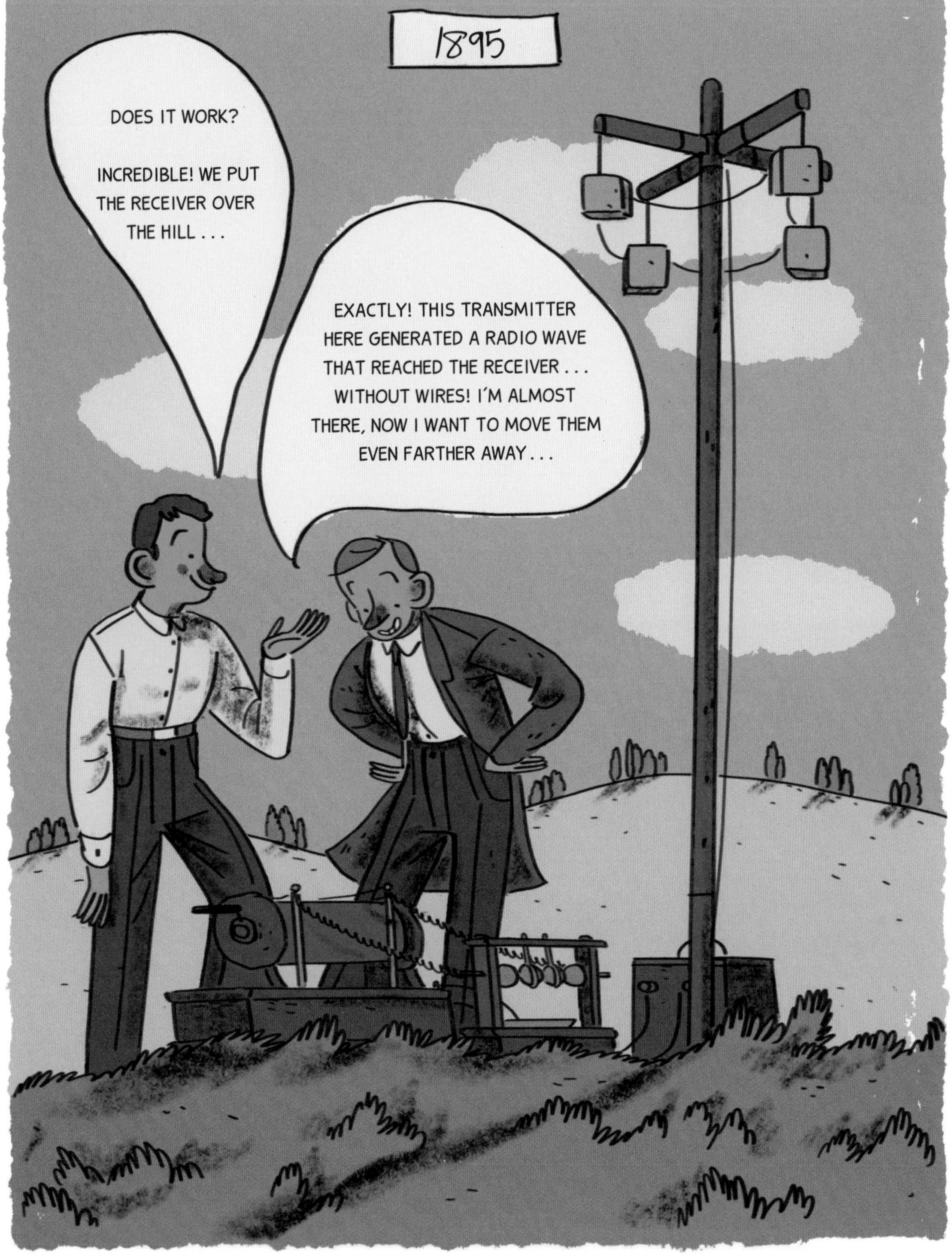
1895
DOES IT WORK?
INCREDIBLE! WE PUT THE RECEIVER OVER THE HILL . . .
EXACTLY! THIS TRANSMITTER HERE GENERATED A RADIO WAVE THAT REACHED THE RECEIVER . . . WITHOUT WIRES! I'M ALMOST THERE, NOW I WANT TO MOVE THEM EVEN FARTHER AWAY . . .

"In the new era,
thought itself will be
transmitted by radio."
Guglielmo Marconi

On the night of December 12, 1901, Guglielmo managed to send a signal from England to a receiver in Canada, which was a distance of 2,200 miles!

"This demonstrates that radio waves can be absorbed by Earth's surface and reemitted!" Marconi mused.

"Impossible," replied other scientists. "Electromagnetic waves [which radio waves are a type of] travel only in a straight line . . . "

" . . . but Earth is round!" added another. "To send radio waves from England to Canada, one of these two theories would have to be wrong."

In reality, the only mistake was in Marconi's explanation of the phenomenon. He had not demonstrated a new property of radio waves: He had just discovered the ionosphere. Too bad he didn't know that at the time!

The ionosphere acts like a mirror surrounding Earth that reflects electromagnetic waves longer than 600 feet and is located very high above Earth's surface. The waves sent by Marconi from England bounced off the ionosphere and, thanks to these movements, they managed to get to Canada!

MISTAKES CAN HAPPEN WHILE LEARNING SOMETHING NEW.

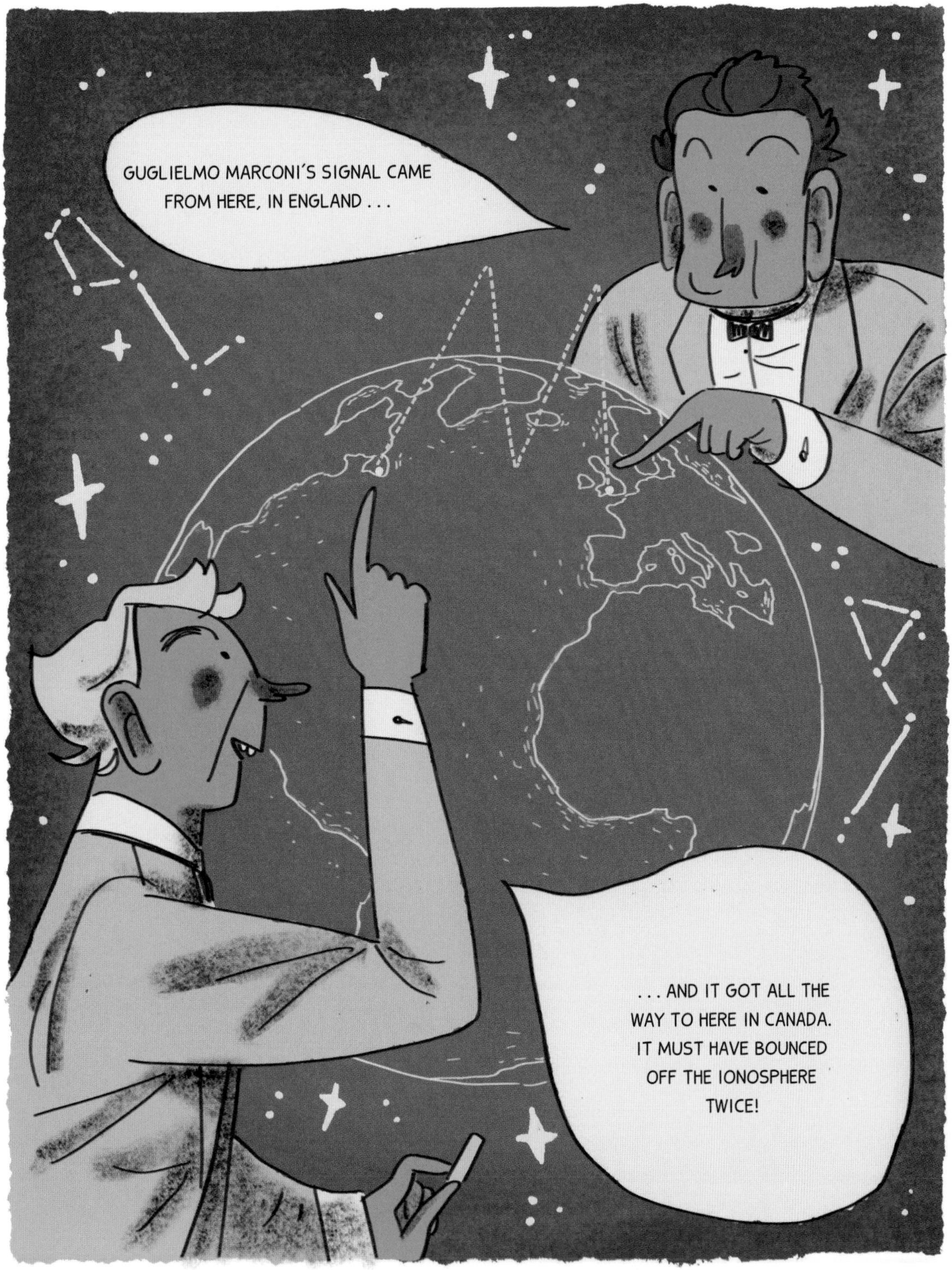
GUGLIELMO MARCONI'S SIGNAL CAME FROM HERE, IN ENGLAND . . .
. . . AND IT GOT ALL THE WAY TO HERE IN CANADA. IT MUST HAVE BOUNCED OFF THE IONOSPHERE TWICE!

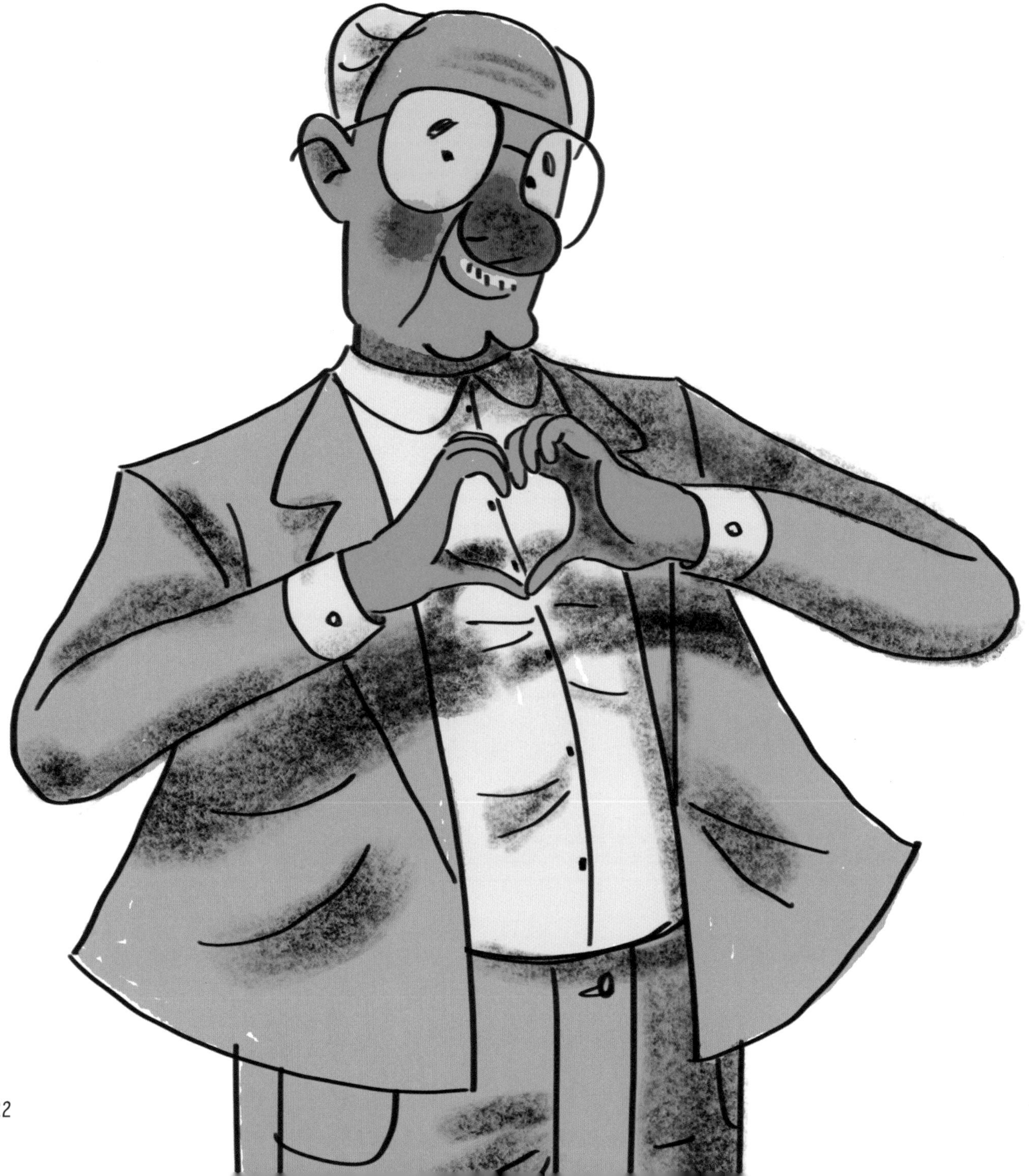

Wilson Greatbatch

Wilson Greatbatch loved understanding how things work.

Wilson Greatbatch was born September 6, 1919, in Buffalo, New York. When the Second World War broke out, he left his studies and offered his help in radio communications, where he had been experimenting for some time. He became aviation chief radio telegraph operator and was honorably discharged in 1945. But Wilson loved studying and understanding things, so in 1950, he graduated with a degree in electrical engineering. He found work on a farm where animal behavior was studied, and it was there that he first heard about a phenomenon he did not know anything about: heart attacks.

The heart normally receives electrical impulses that cause it to contract and pump blood through the body. During a heart attack, these impulses stop.

So, Wilson came up with an idea for a machine capable of restarting the heart. He studied hard and made numerous attempts until he perfected it. It was called a pacemaker, or heart stimulator.

How did Wilson invent the pacemaker?
Turn the page to find out!

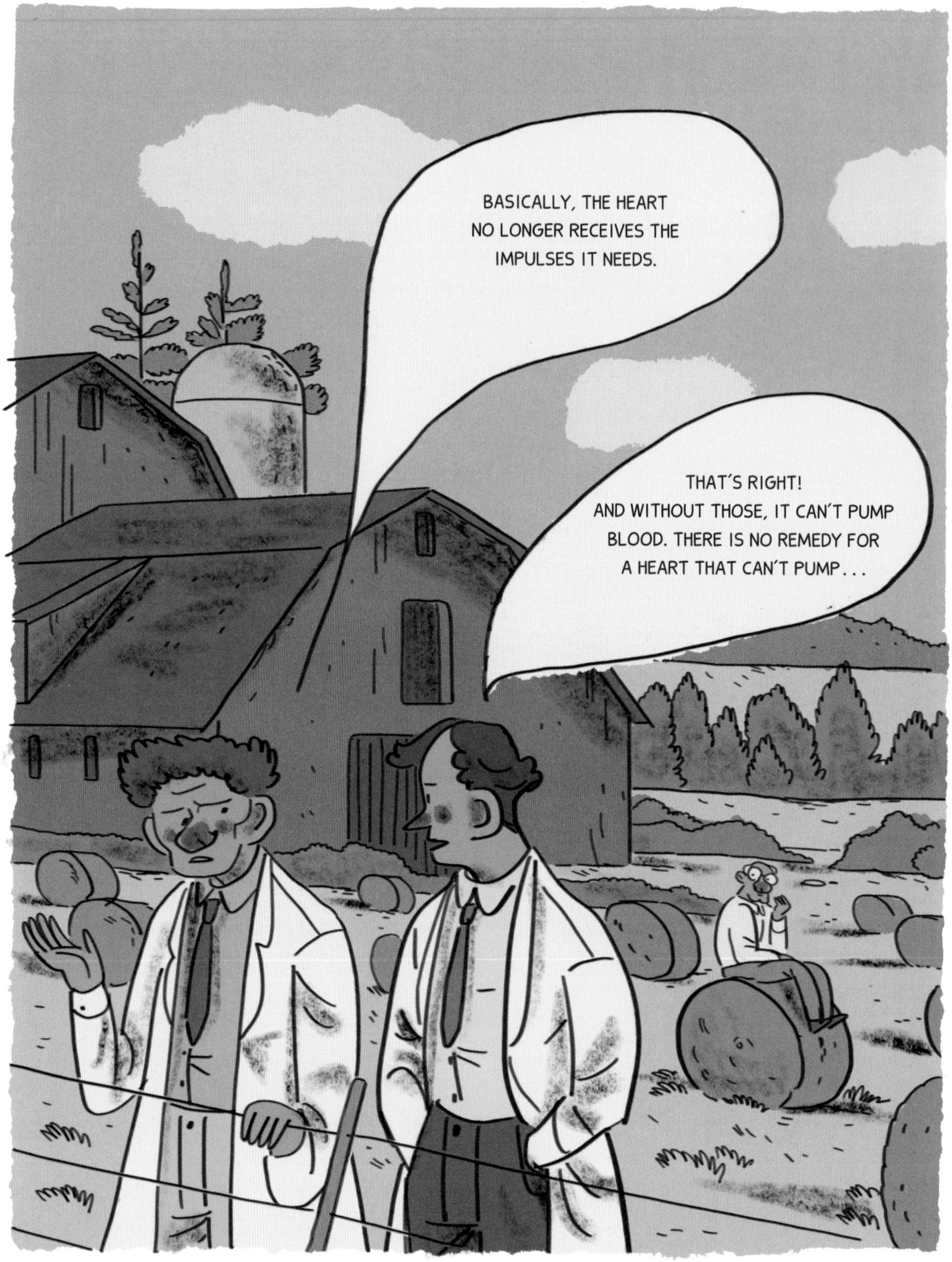
BASICALLY, THE HEART NO LONGER RECEIVES THE IMPULSES IT NEEDS.
THAT'S RIGHT! AND WITHOUT THOSE, IT CAN'T PUMP BLOOD. THERE IS NO REMEDY FOR A HEART THAT CAN'T PUMP...

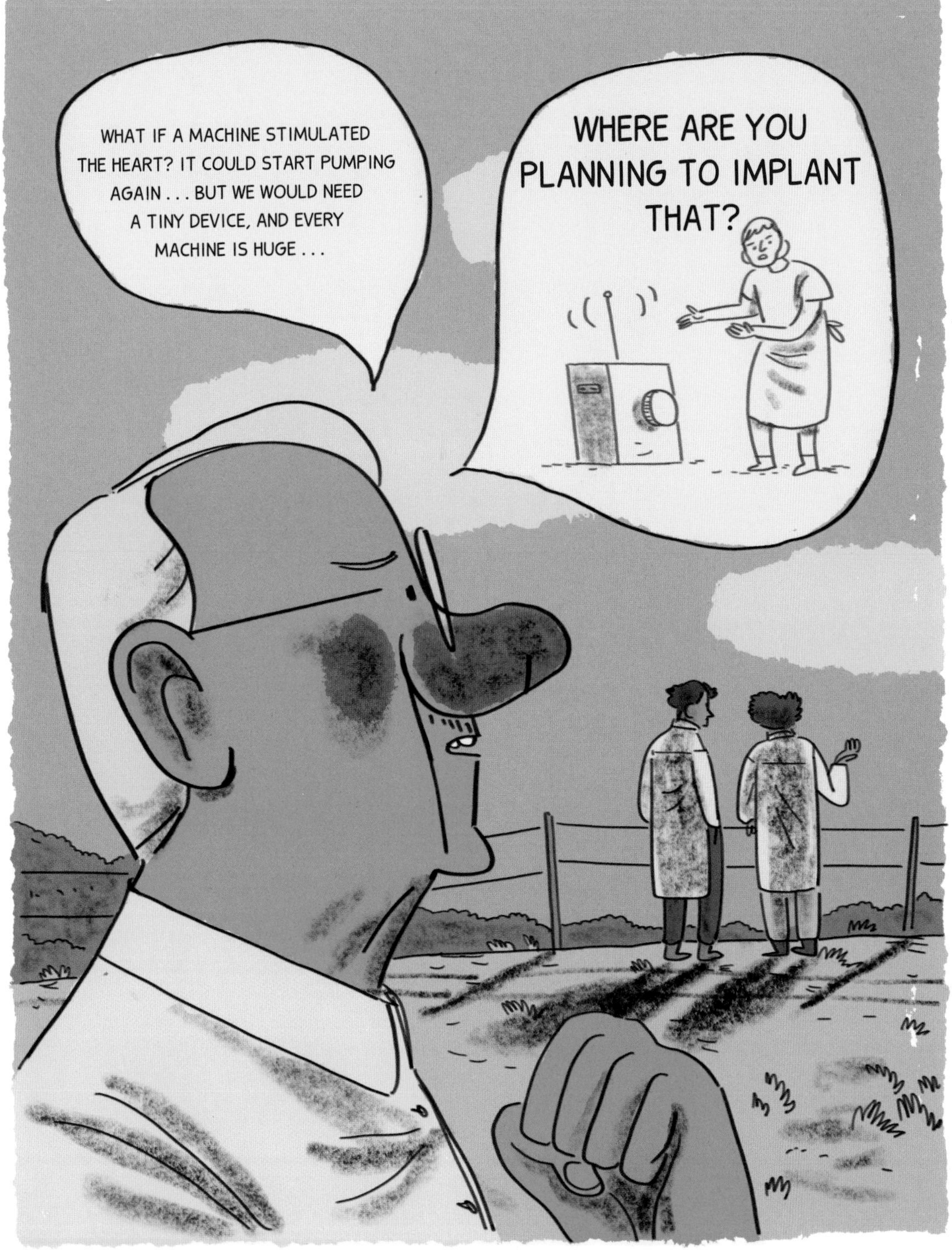
WHAT IF A MACHINE STIMULATED THE HEART? IT COULD START PUMPING AGAIN . . . BUT WE WOULD NEED A TINY DEVICE, AND EVERY MACHINE IS HUGE . . .
WHERE ARE YOU PLANNING TO IMPLANT THAT?

"Failure is a learning experience, and the guy who has never failed has never done anything."

Wilson Greatbatch

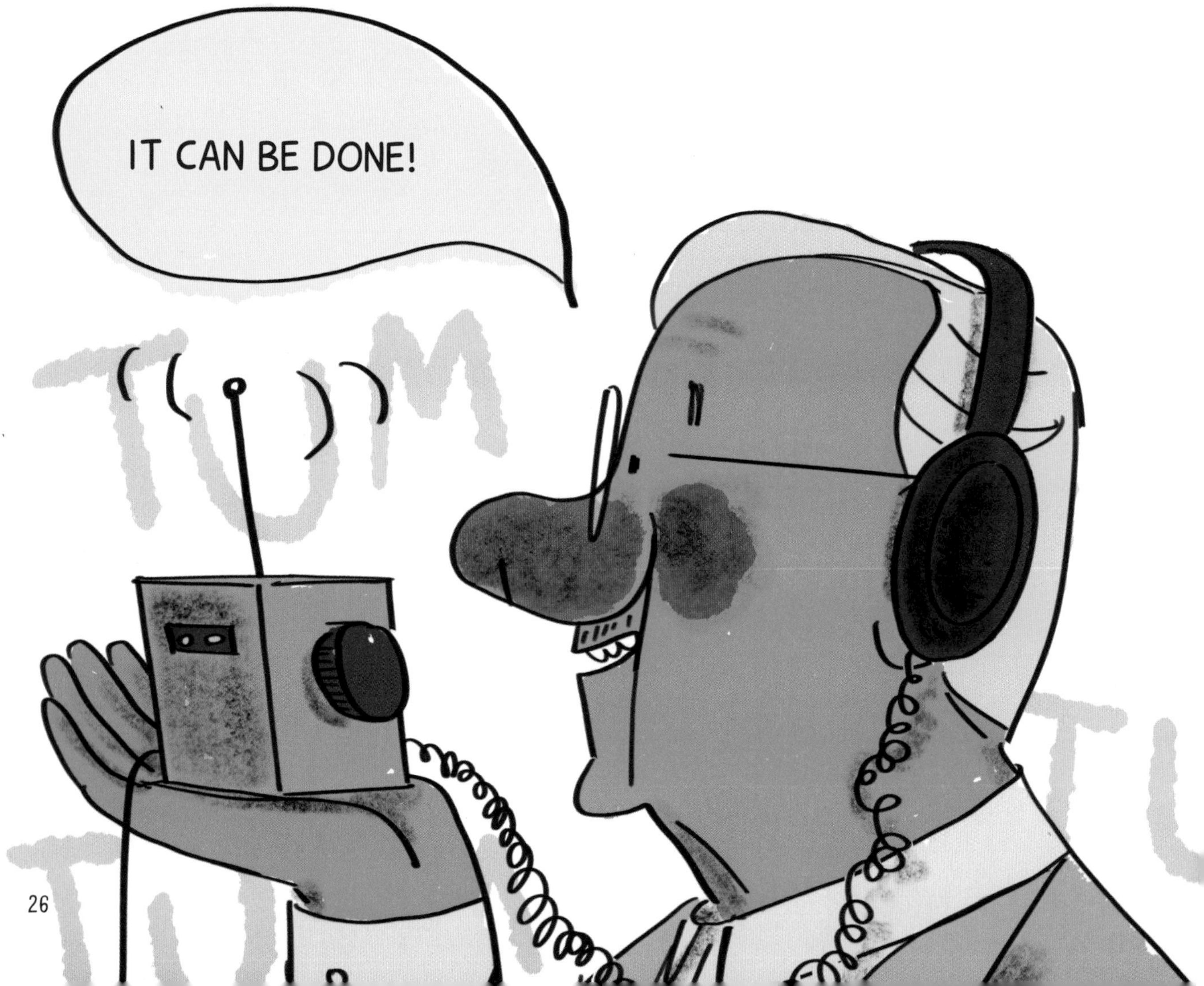
IT CAN BE DONE!
TUM

In 1956, Wilson was trying to create a machine capable of recording the rhythm of the heart. But he made a mistake—he added a wrong electrical component. The device did not record the sound of the heartbeat but instead created independent electrical impulses. It was not going exactly as he hoped, and yet . . .

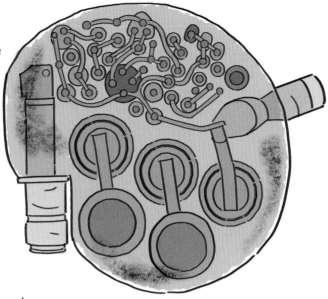

Wilson listened. The new device produced a sound similar to that of a healthy heart with a steady and uninterrupted rhythm.

"This is how it can be done!" he thought.

He now had a different idea. For some time he had been thinking about how to help those affected by a heart attack, and that device designed by mistake could do the job! By connecting it to a weak heart, it could help pump blood smoothly . . . he had just discovered how to make a pacemaker!

Sure, it took him a lot of attempts to make the device small enough to fit inside a person's chest, but then in 1960, the first pacemaker was implanted in a human patient, Henry Hennafeld, allowing him to live out the rest of his life.

IF YOU PAY ATTENTION TO A MISTAKE, YOU CAN FIND NEW PATHS.

Wilson Greatbatch

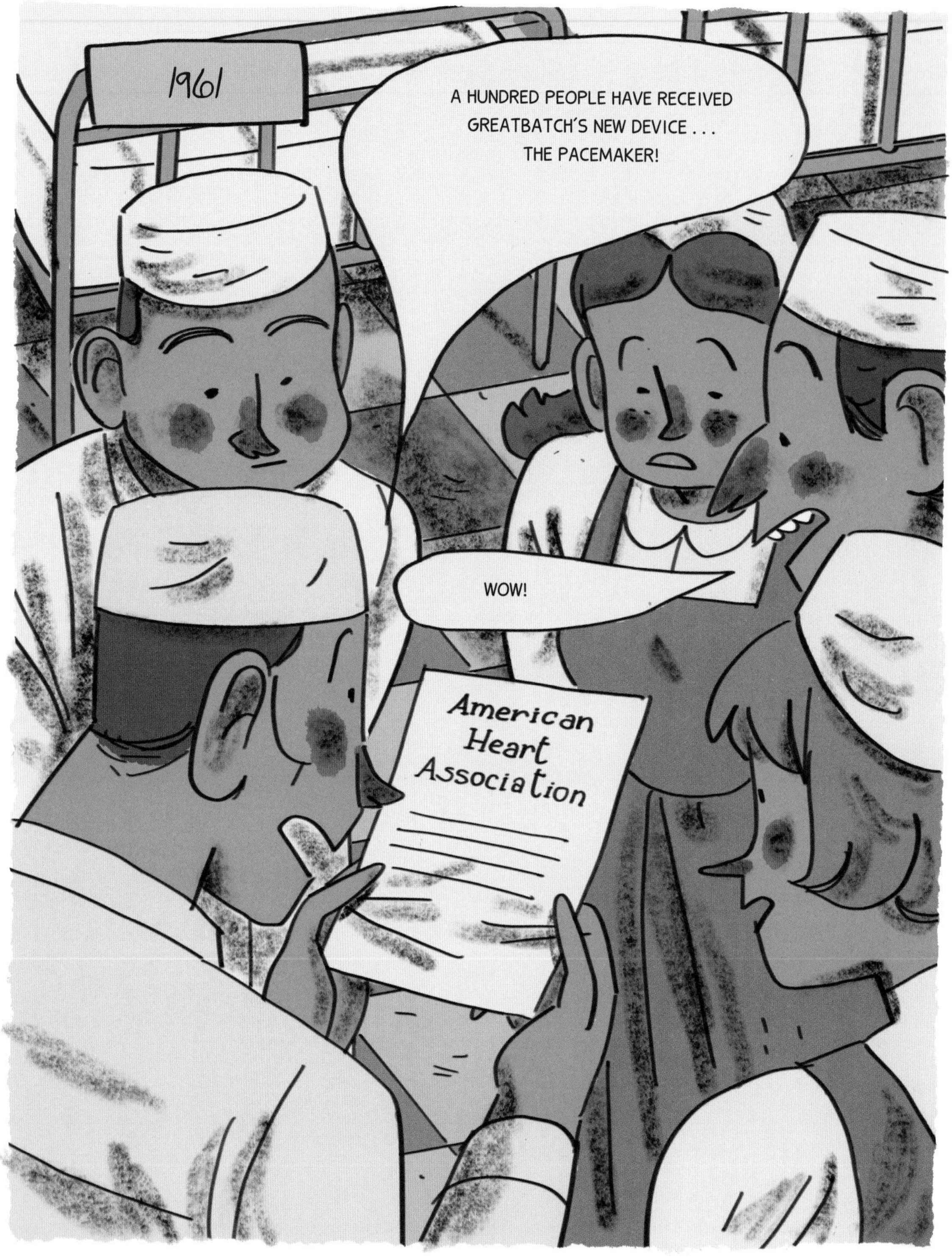
1961
A HUNDRED PEOPLE HAVE RECEIVED GREATBATCH'S NEW DEVICE . . . THE PACEMAKER!
WOW!
American Heart Association

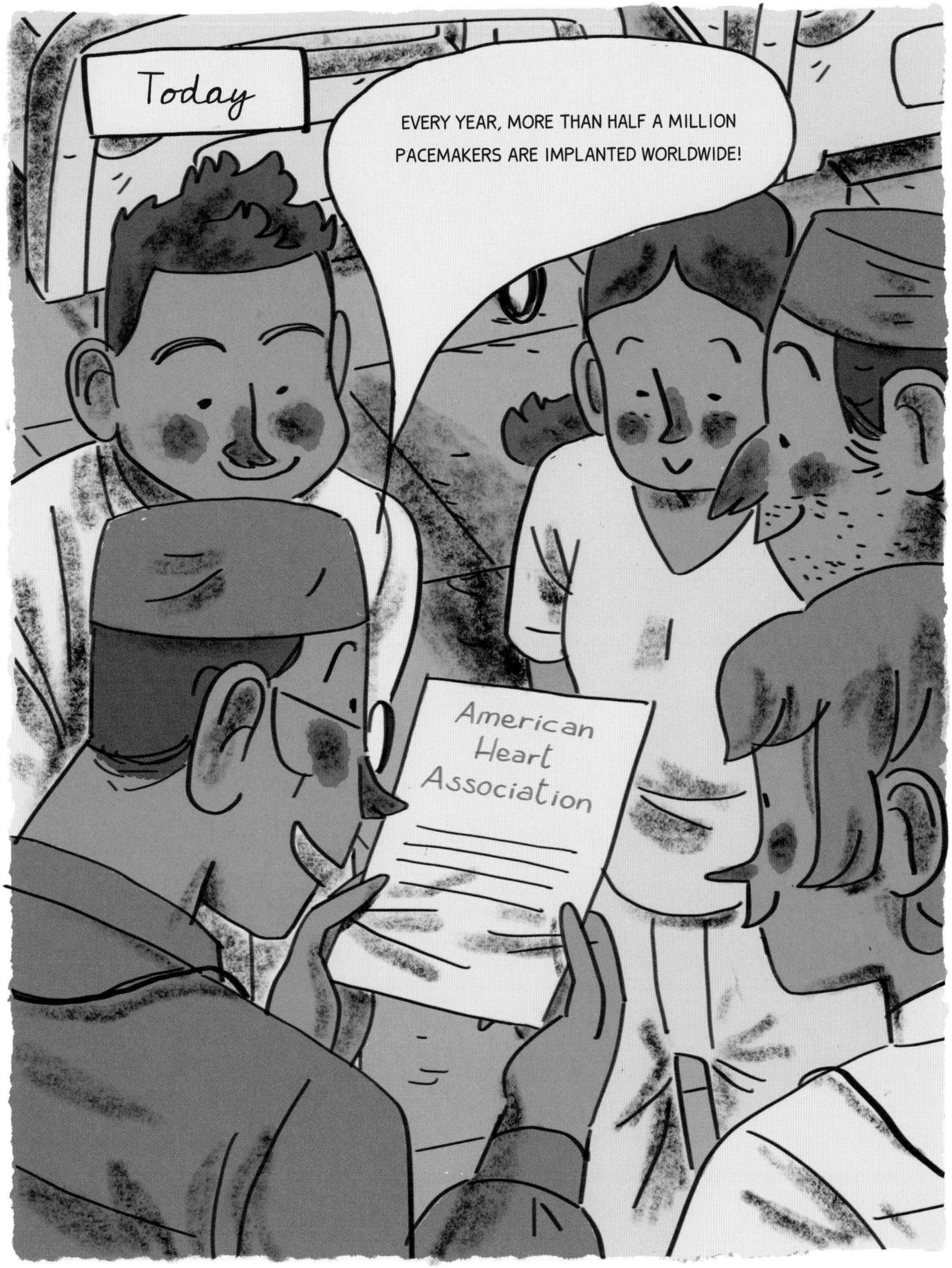
Today
EVERY YEAR, MORE THAN HALF A MILLION PACEMAKERS ARE IMPLANTED WORLDWIDE!
American Heart Association

James Dyson

**James Dyson was certain that technology
could be improved.**

James Dyson was born on May 2, 1947, in Cromer, England. As a boy he studied a lot. After graduation he attended the Byam Shaw School of Art in London, then the Royal College of Art, where he discovered that engineering could also be creative. In 1974, he founded a company to produce his first invention: a wheelbarrow that could be easily moved.

Four years later, he had an idea destined to change the course of household appliance history: a new bagless technology for vacuum cleaners. Dyson was excited and worked hard to perfect it.

Unfortunately, traditional appliance manufacturers were not interested in his invention. They believed that vacuum cleaners worked just fine with the bag! But Dyson was the stubborn type.

Keep reading to find out just what James Dyson did.

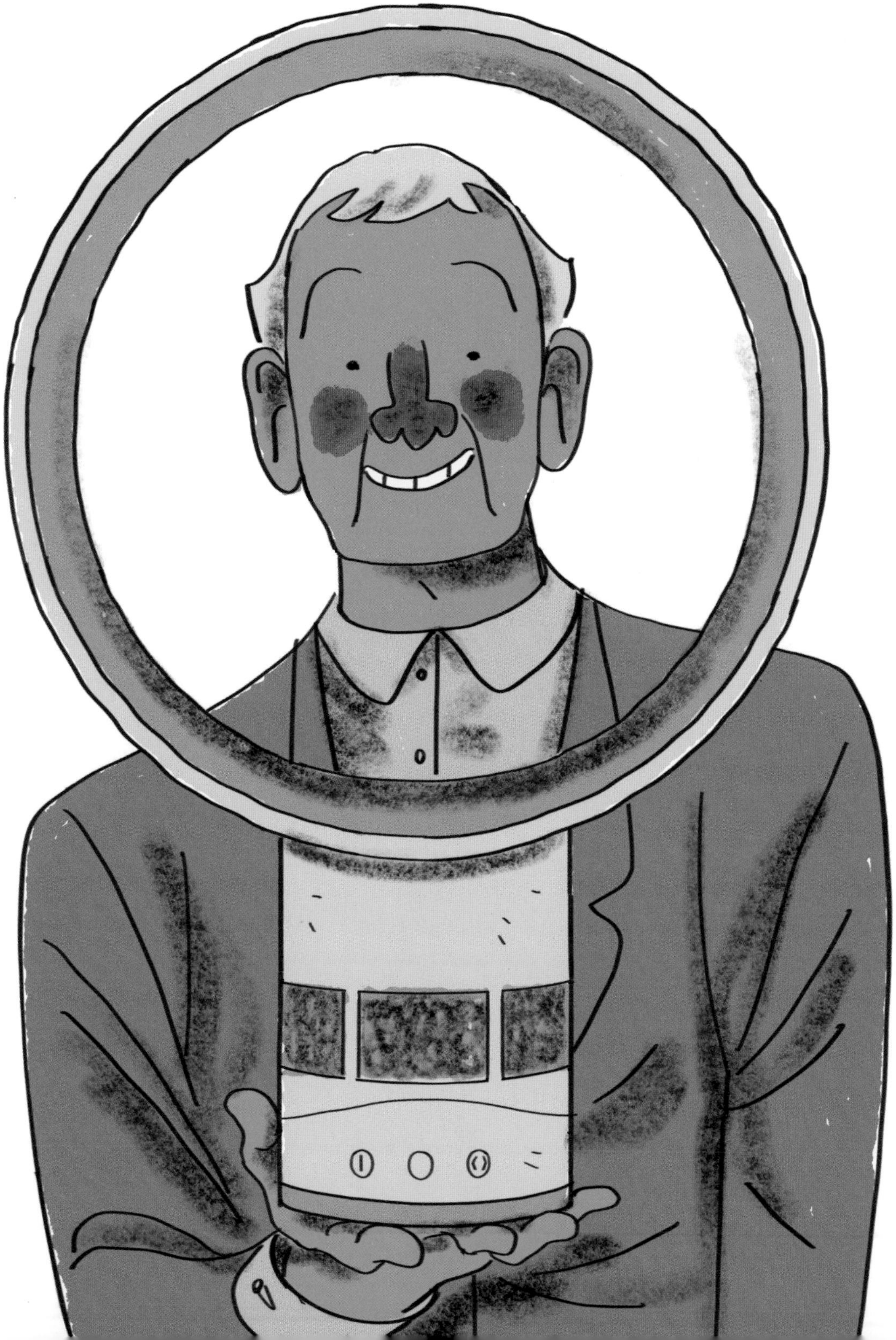

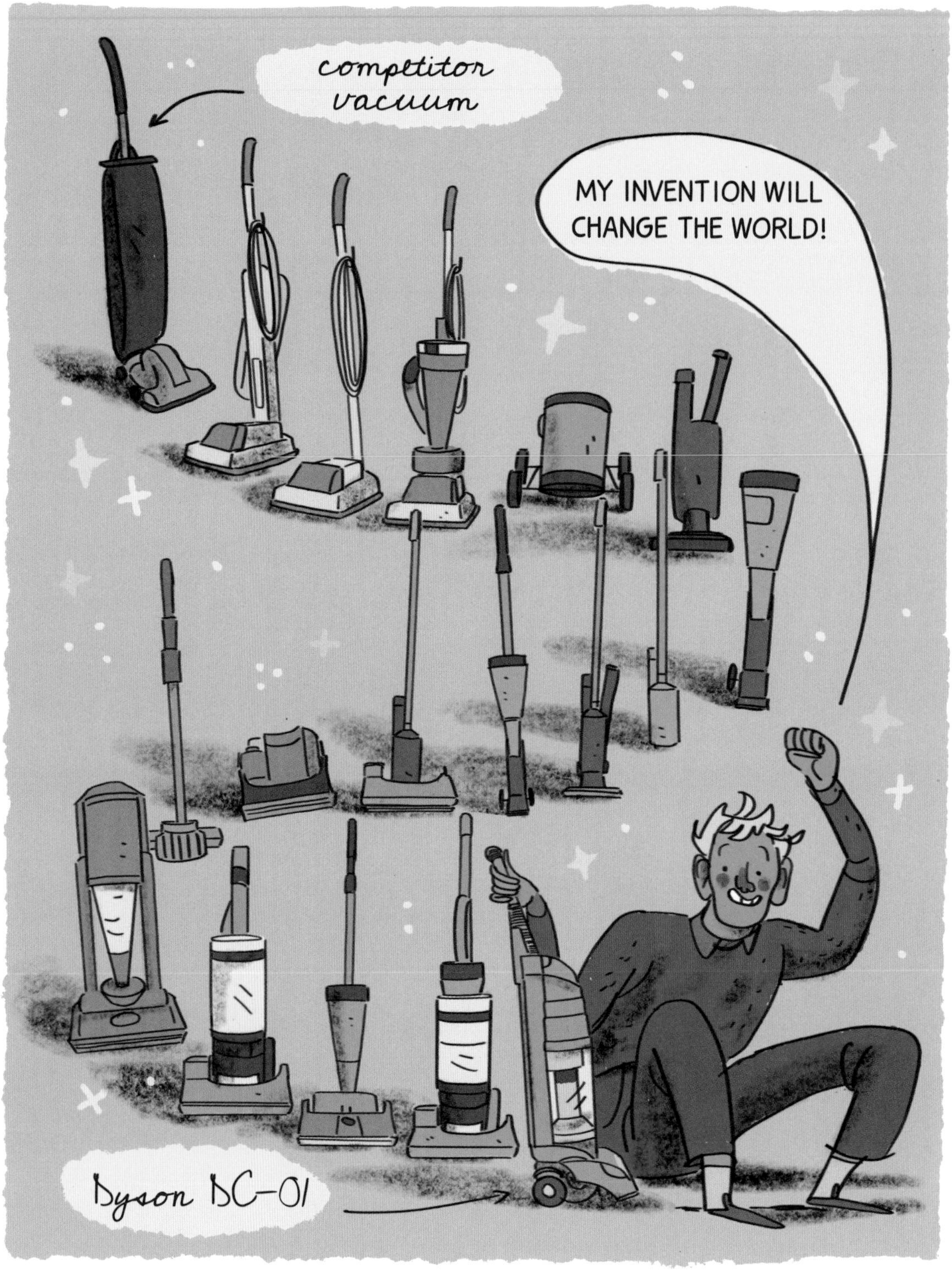
competitor vacuum
MY INVENTION WILL CHANGE THE WORLD!
Dyson DC-01

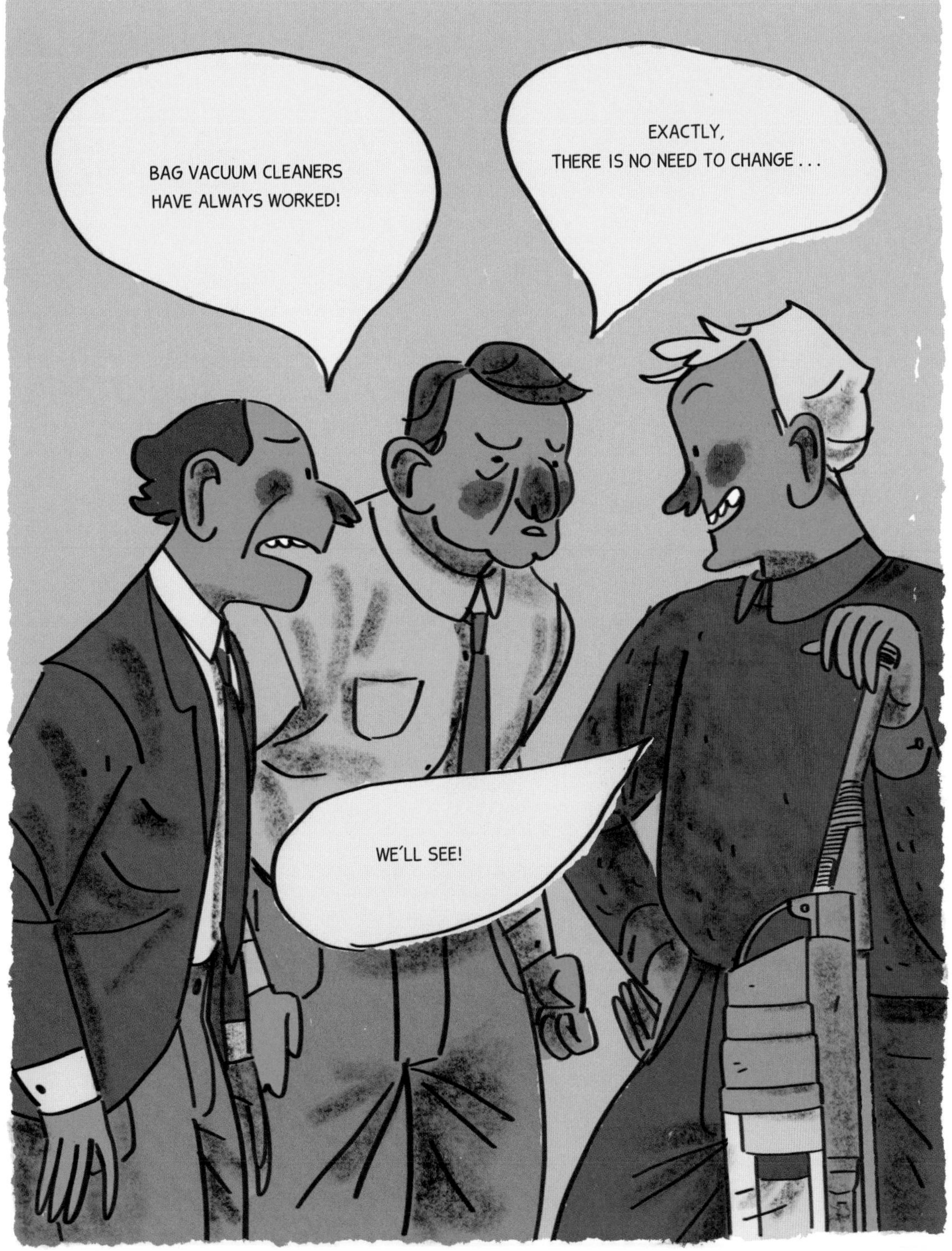
BAG VACUUM CLEANERS HAVE ALWAYS WORKED!
EXACTLY, THERE IS NO NEED TO CHANGE . . .
WE´LL SEE!

"Enjoy failure and learn from it. You can never learn from success."
James Dyson

Although bag cleaners had been used in the past, they weren't always efficient. James got the idea for his bagless vacuum when another vacuum cleaner suddenly stopped working—the bag was clogged, and the vacuum cleaner wouldn't start again.

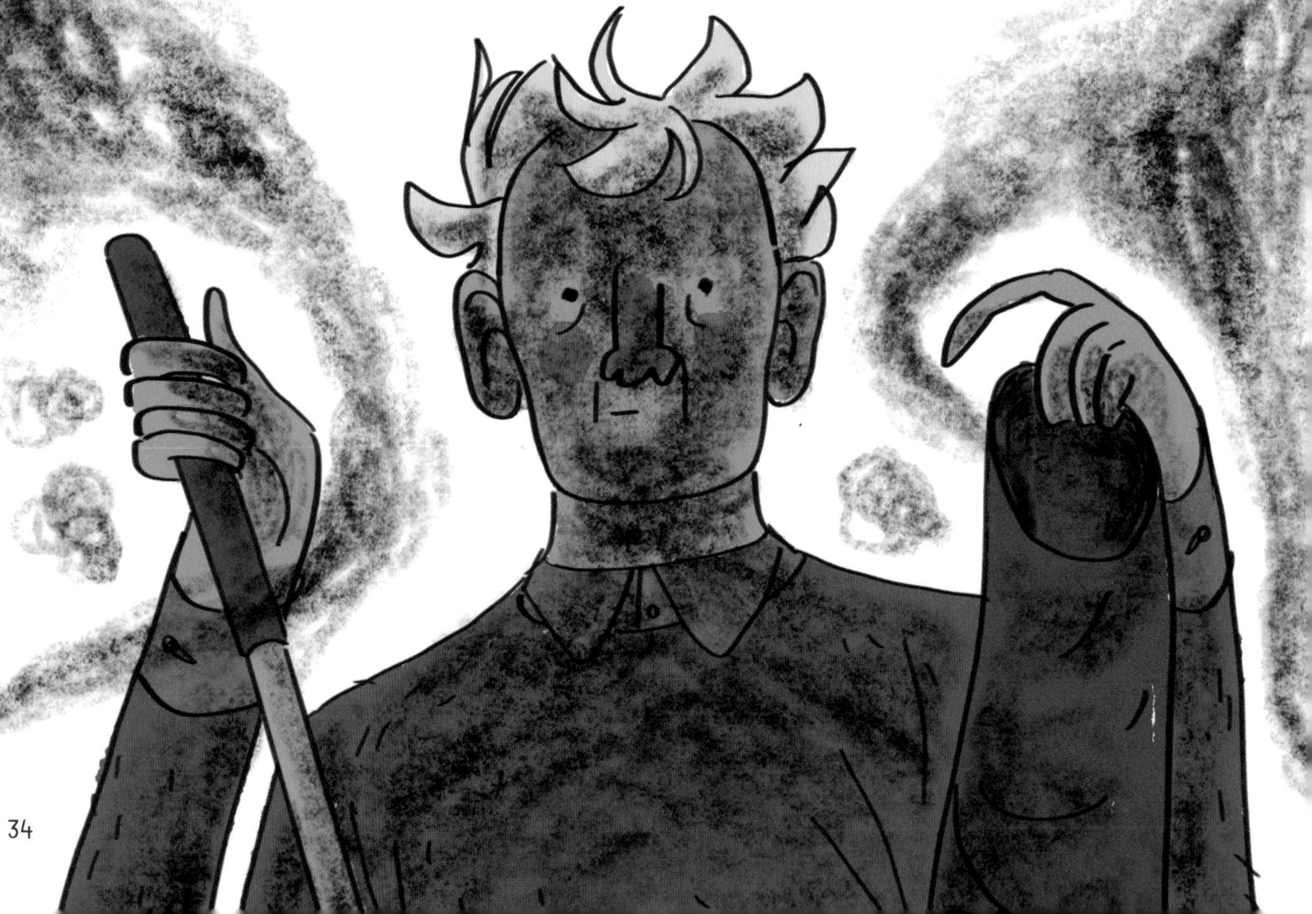

Dyson remembered what he had seen in a sawmill some time before: They used a technology called "cyclones" that separated the particles of sawdust from the air. "Why don't I try it in my old vacuum cleaner?" he thought.

He removed the clogged bag and substituted it with a prototype cyclone filter he made out of rough cardboard. He used the modified vacuum cleaner in one room and picked up more dust than before! Of course he now had to perfect the idea, so he got to work.

A full 15 years and 5,126 prototypes later, his first vacuum cleaner was ready. That's right: 15 years of mistakes! And it wasn't over yet.

After the first model was completed in 1993, over 30 others were created, improving on the previous ones. Every mistake has allowed Dyson to perfect the efficiency, speed, and materials of his vacuum cleaners. Yet at the beginning no one believed in his invention. Bag vacuum cleaners had always worked, so why change? Dyson decided to produce his bagless vacuums himself and created the company that still bears his name today! He even set up the James Dyson Award, an international award that celebrates the creators of new problem-solving inventions.

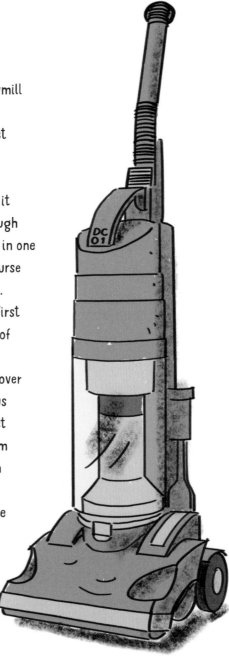

MAKING MISTAKES AND NOT GIVING UP, WHILE BELIEVING IN YOURSELF, CAN GO A LONG WAY.

James Dyson

Now Dyson's company makes tons of helpful inventions!

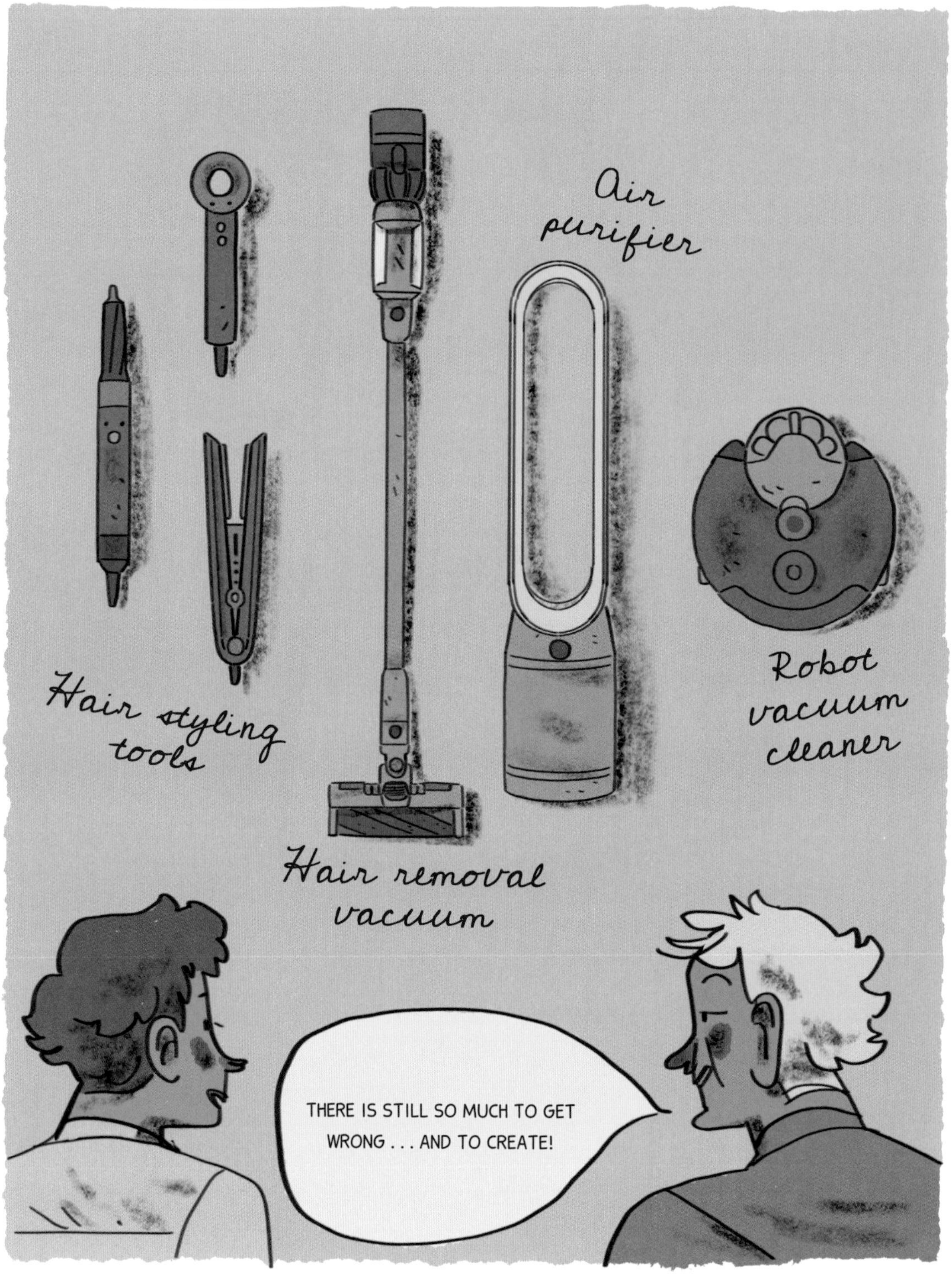

Hair styling tools
Air purifier
Robot vacuum cleaner
Hair removal vacuum
THERE IS STILL SO MUCH TO GET WRONG . . . AND TO CREATE!

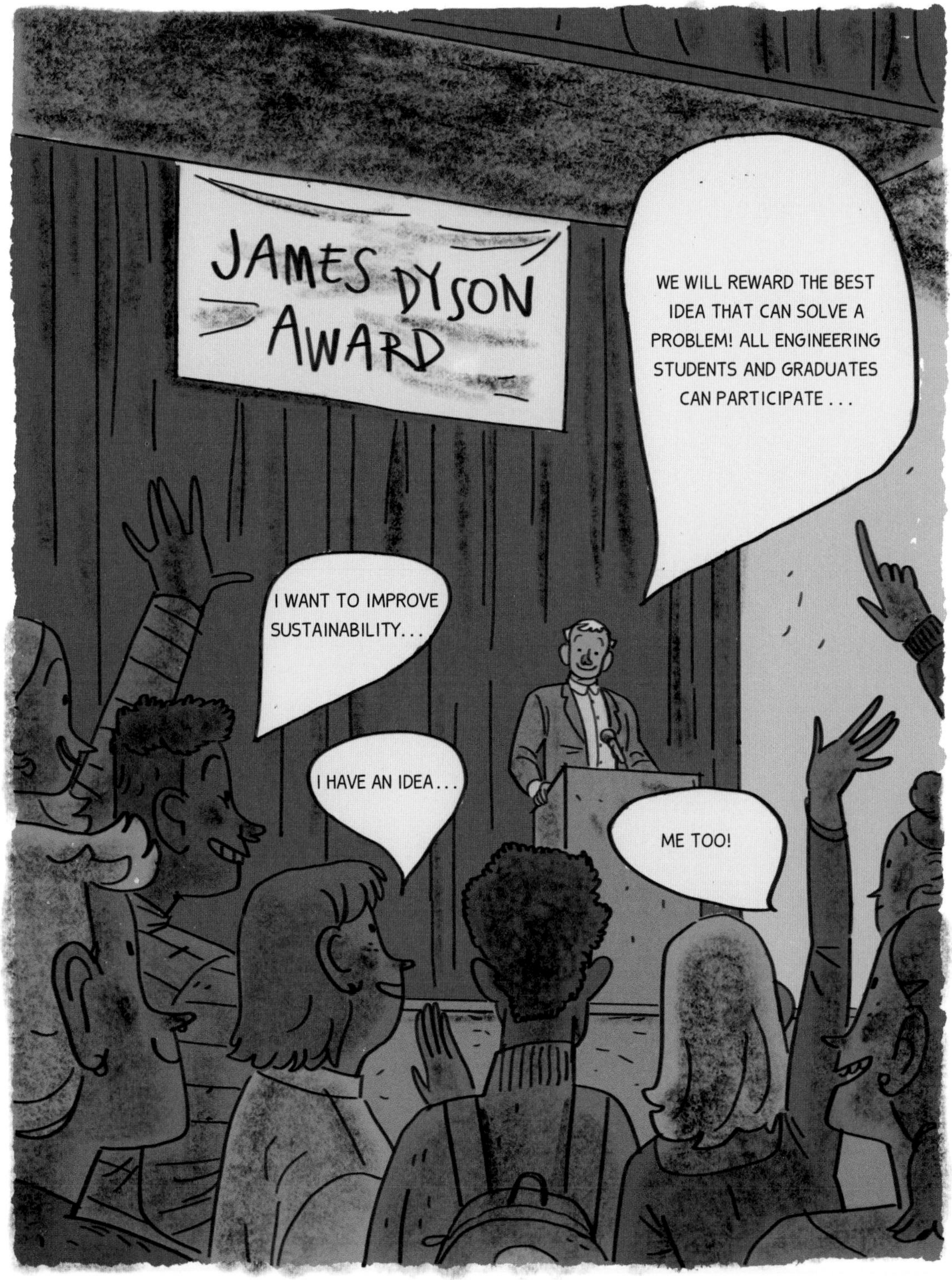
JAMES DYSON AWARD
WE WILL REWARD THE BEST IDEA THAT CAN SOLVE A PROBLEM! ALL ENGINEERING STUDENTS AND GRADUATES CAN PARTICIPATE . . .
I WANT TO IMPROVE SUSTAINABILITY. . .
I HAVE AN IDEA. . .
ME TOO!

Margarete Steiff

**Margarete Steiff was an iconic inventor who loved to
make children smile and invented the teddy bear.**

Margarete Steiff was born on July 24, 1847, in Giengen an der Brenz, Germany.
She was barely a year and a half old when she fell ill and had to navigate
the rest of her life with a wheelchair. Even though her right hand moved with
difficulty, Margarete attended a school for sewing, her great passion, and at
17, she became a seamstress. Full of energy, she worked in her older sisters'
shop. Then her father transformed the Steiff house into a workshop, and
Margarete had her own tailoring business!

Margarete found that she liked a material called felt, a fabric made from
treated animal fibers. She started using it and, at age 30, she opened her
first shop, where she made clothes and objects for the home.

But how did Margarete invent the teddy bear?
You're about to find out!

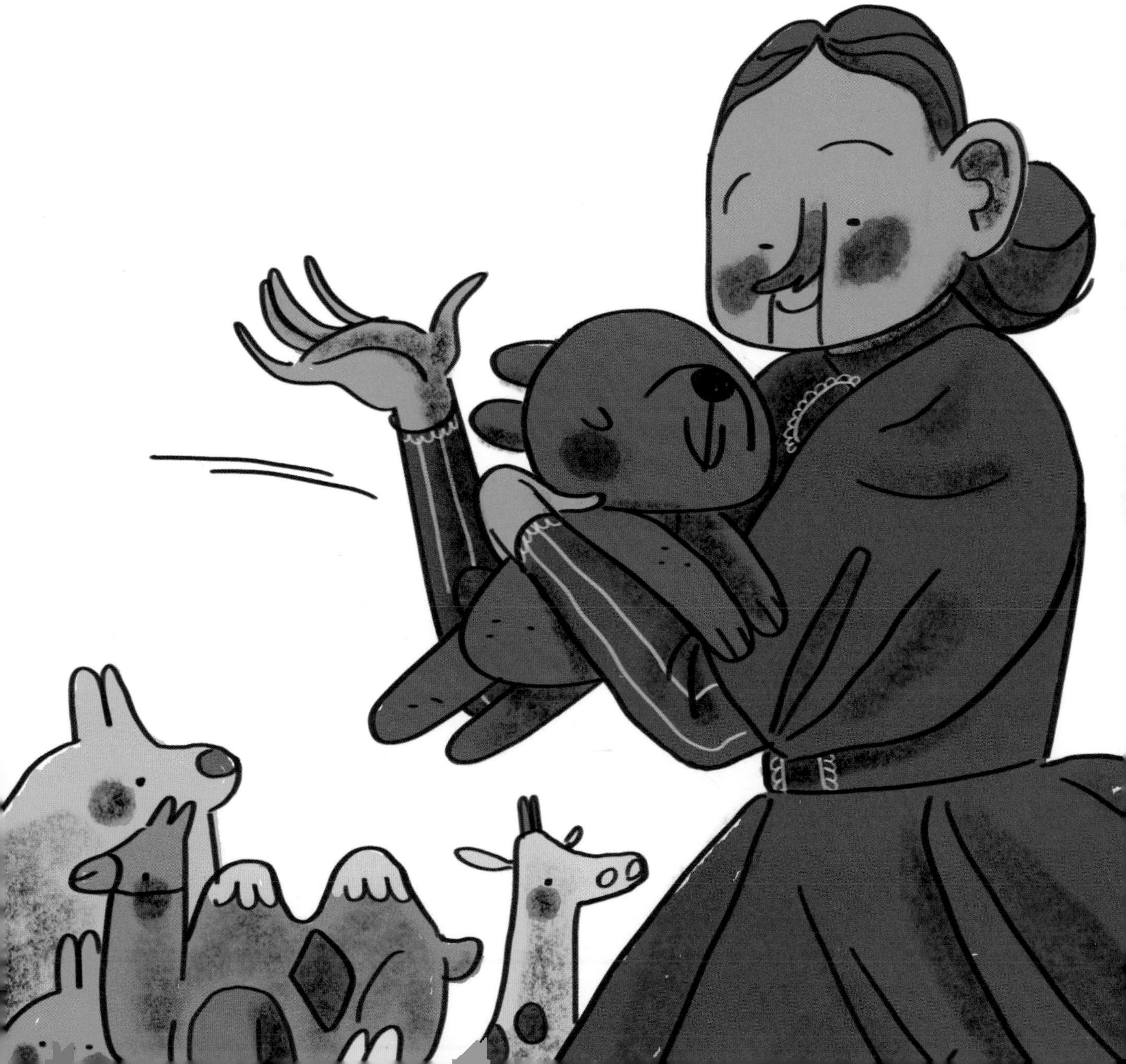

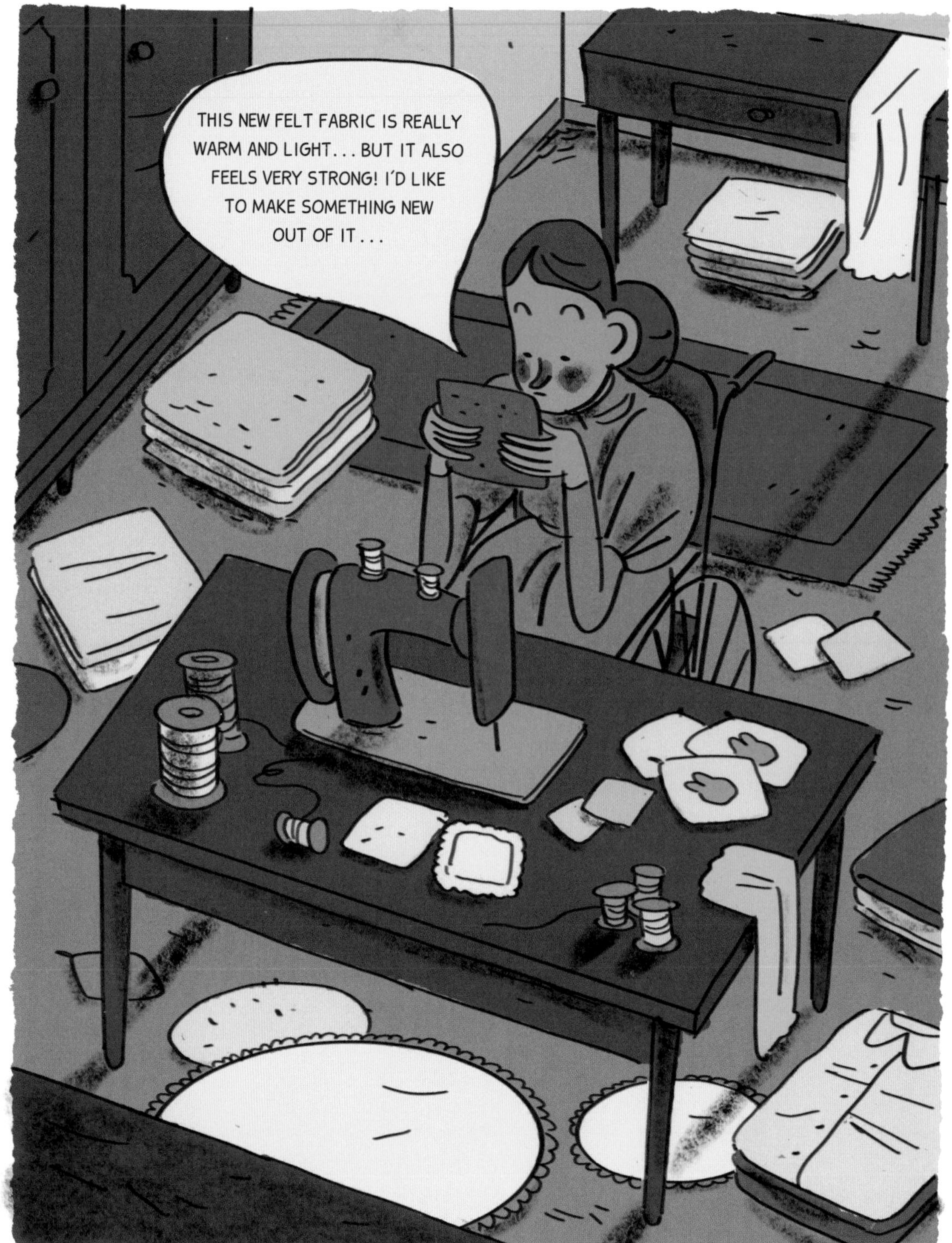
THIS NEW FELT FABRIC IS REALLY WARM AND LIGHT. . . BUT IT ALSO FEELS VERY STRONG! I'D LIKE TO MAKE SOMETHING NEW OUT OF IT . . .

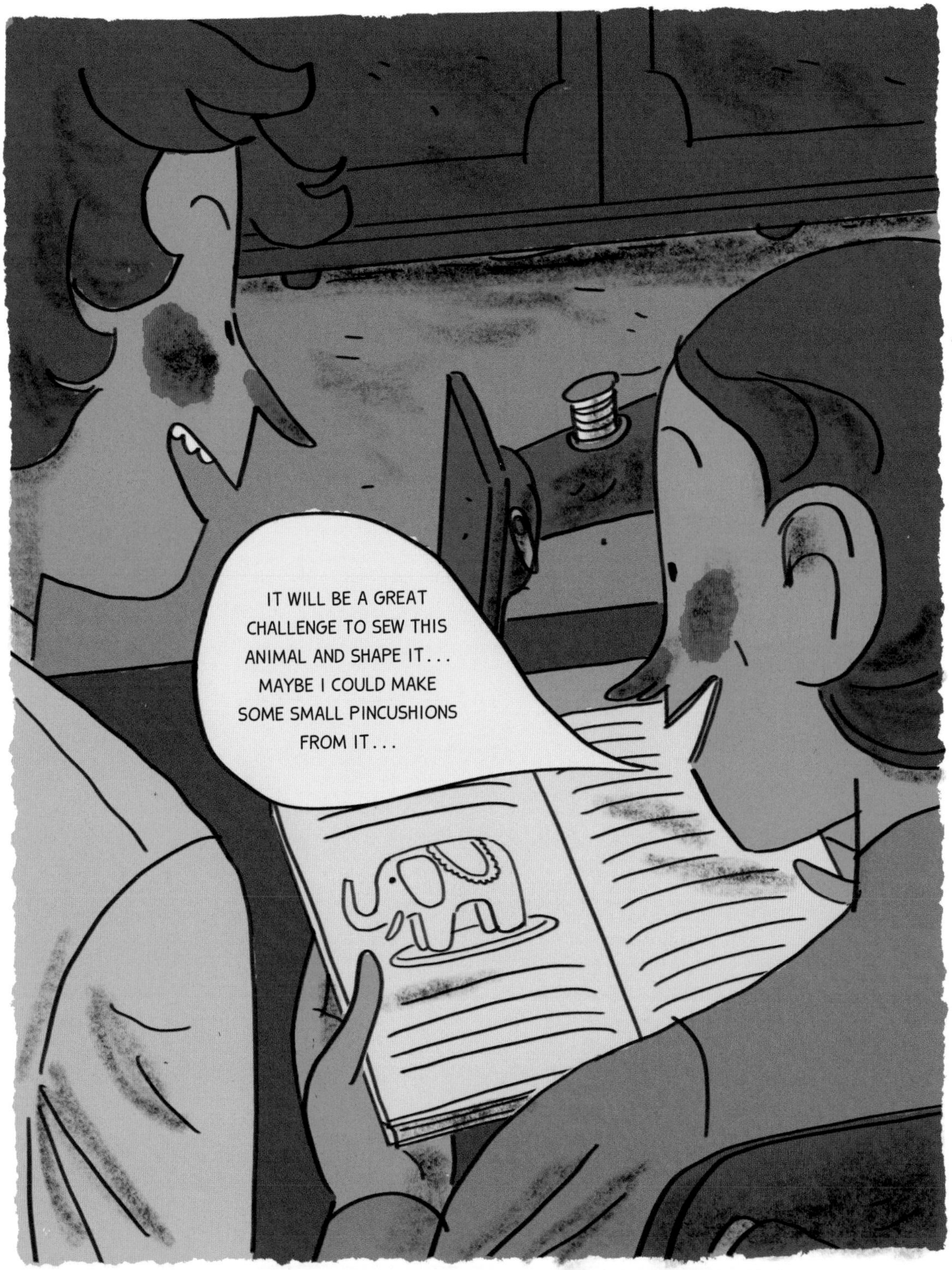
IT WILL BE A GREAT CHALLENGE TO SEW THIS ANIMAL AND SHAPE IT... MAYBE I COULD MAKE SOME SMALL PINCUSHIONS FROM IT...

Margarete's brother, Fritz, encouraged her to make more pincushion elephants. He told her that everyone at the market liked them.

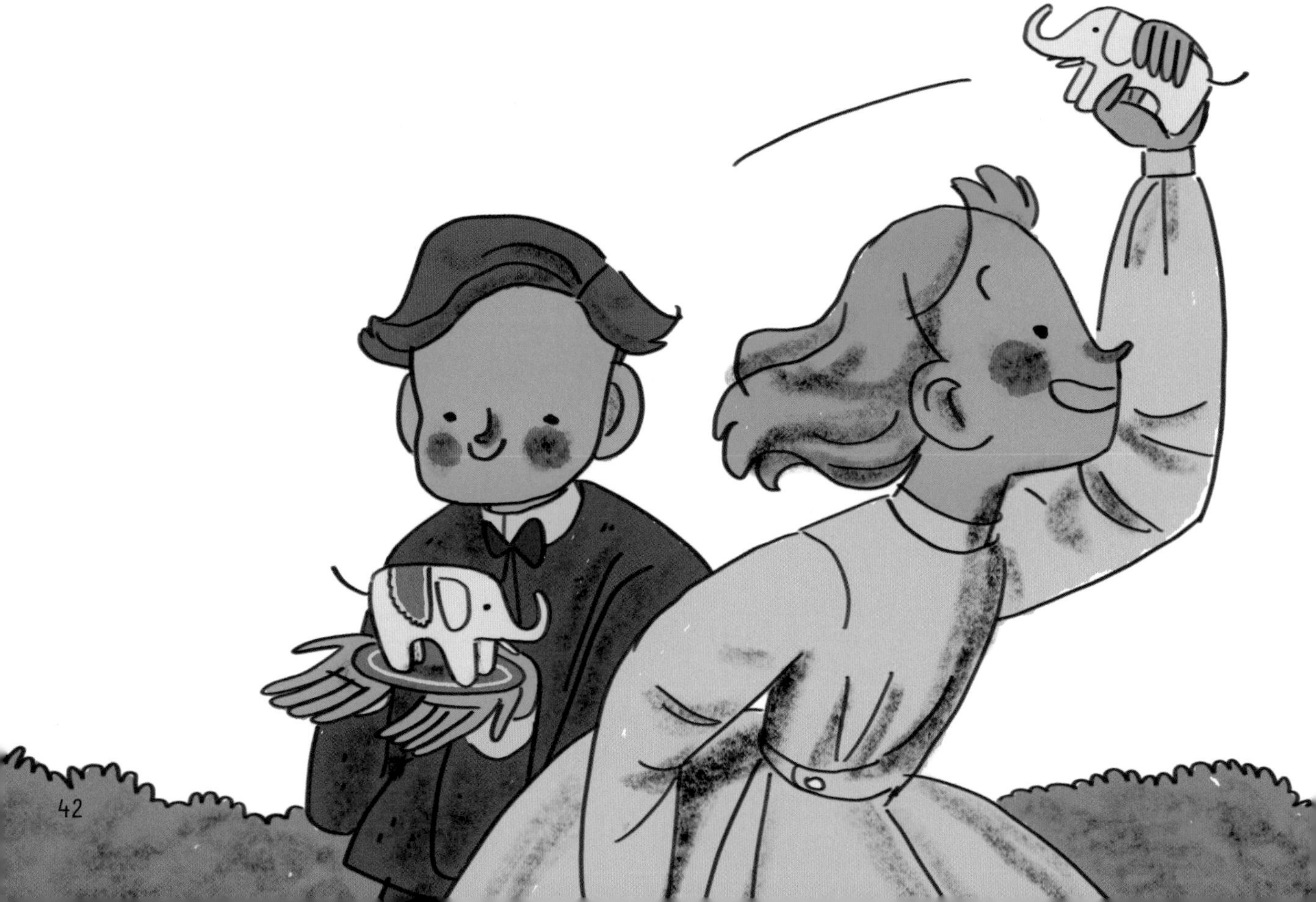

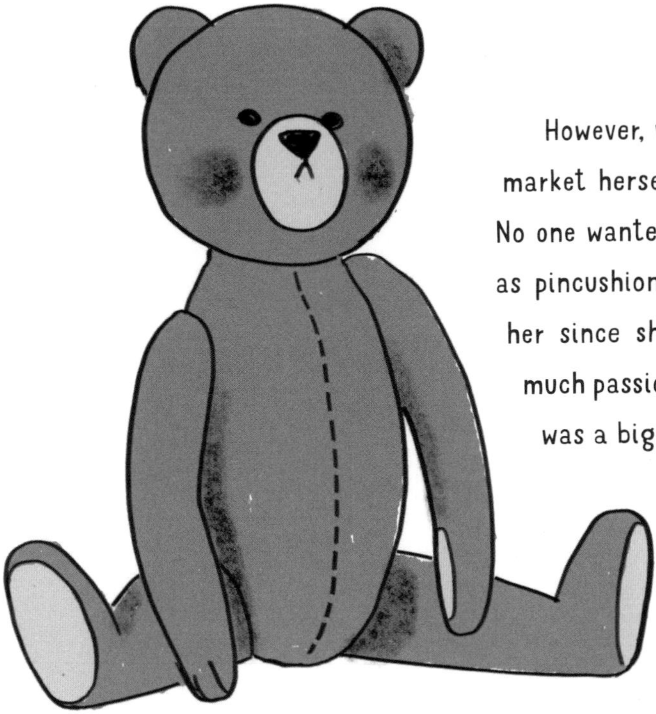

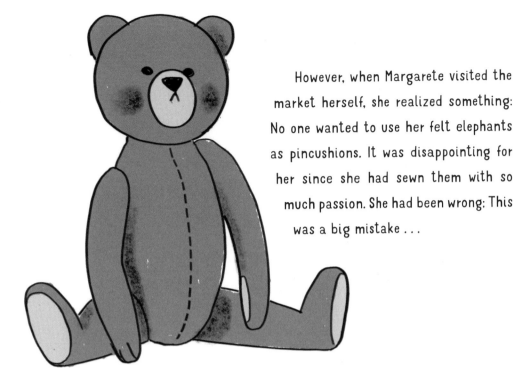

However, when Margarete visited the market herself, she realized something: No one wanted to use her felt elephants as pincushions. It was disappointing for her since she had sewn them with so much passion. She had been wrong: This was a big mistake . . .

Suddenly she heard laughter. Children were chasing each other in the market. She observed them closely and realized that they were holding something she knew very well: her felt elephants. That is why they were so in demand at the market. The children played with them! It was not what she had in mind, yet she realized that she had come up with something precious. From that day on she never stopped creating soft toys and games for children. Then, thanks to her nephew, she ended up creating the teddy bear!

THINGS DON'T ALWAYS WORK THE WAY YOU IMAGINED.
BUT THERE CAN BE A DIFFERENT PURPOSE, PERHAPS A BETTER
ONE: AN ERROR CAN SOMETIMES LEAD SOMEWHERE ELSE.

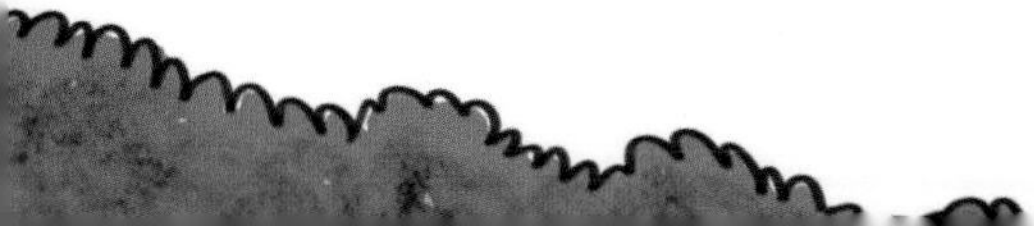

Margarete Steiff

How the teddy bear came to be:

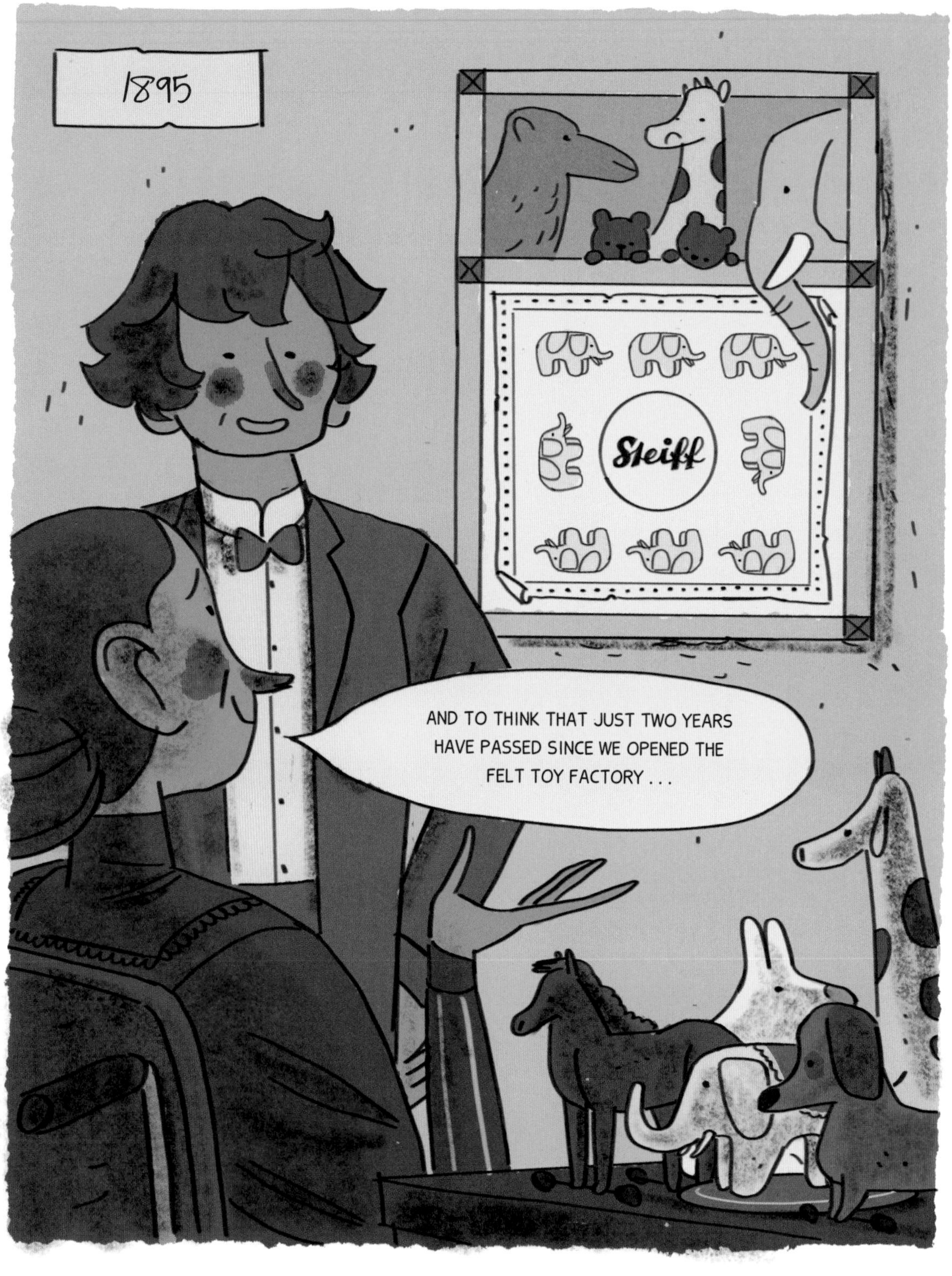
1895
Steiff
AND TO THINK THAT JUST TWO YEARS HAVE PASSED SINCE WE OPENED THE FELT TOY FACTORY . . .

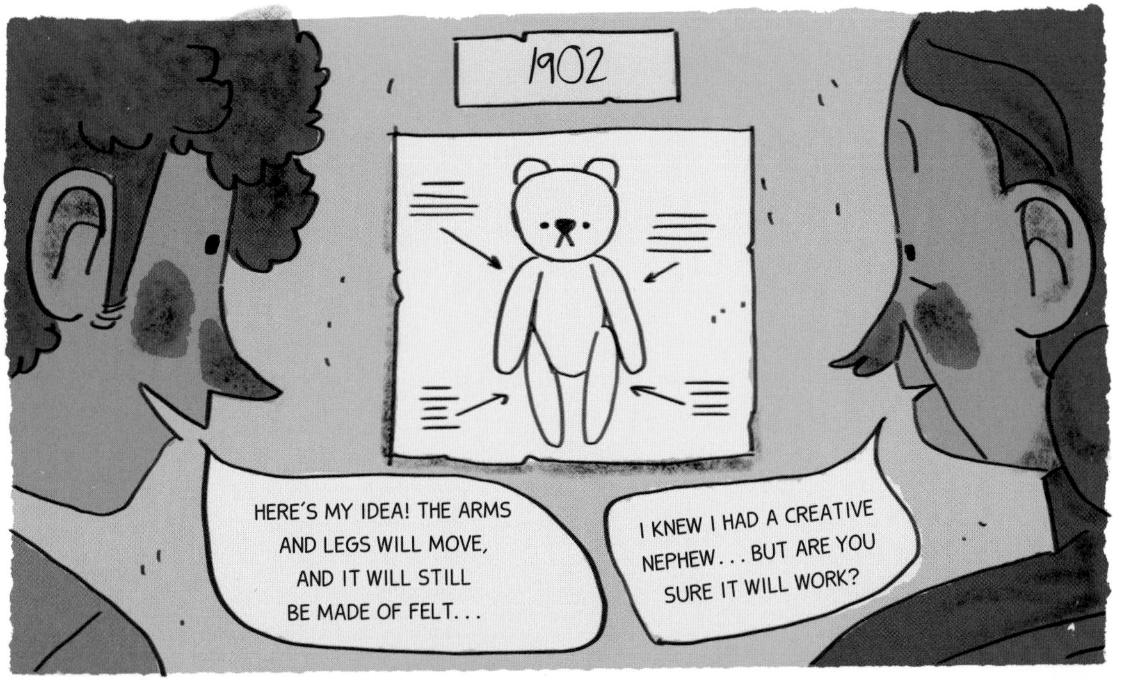
1902
HERE'S MY IDEA! THE ARMS AND LEGS WILL MOVE, AND IT WILL STILL BE MADE OF FELT...
I KNEW I HAD A CREATIVE NEPHEW... BUT ARE YOU SURE IT WILL WORK?

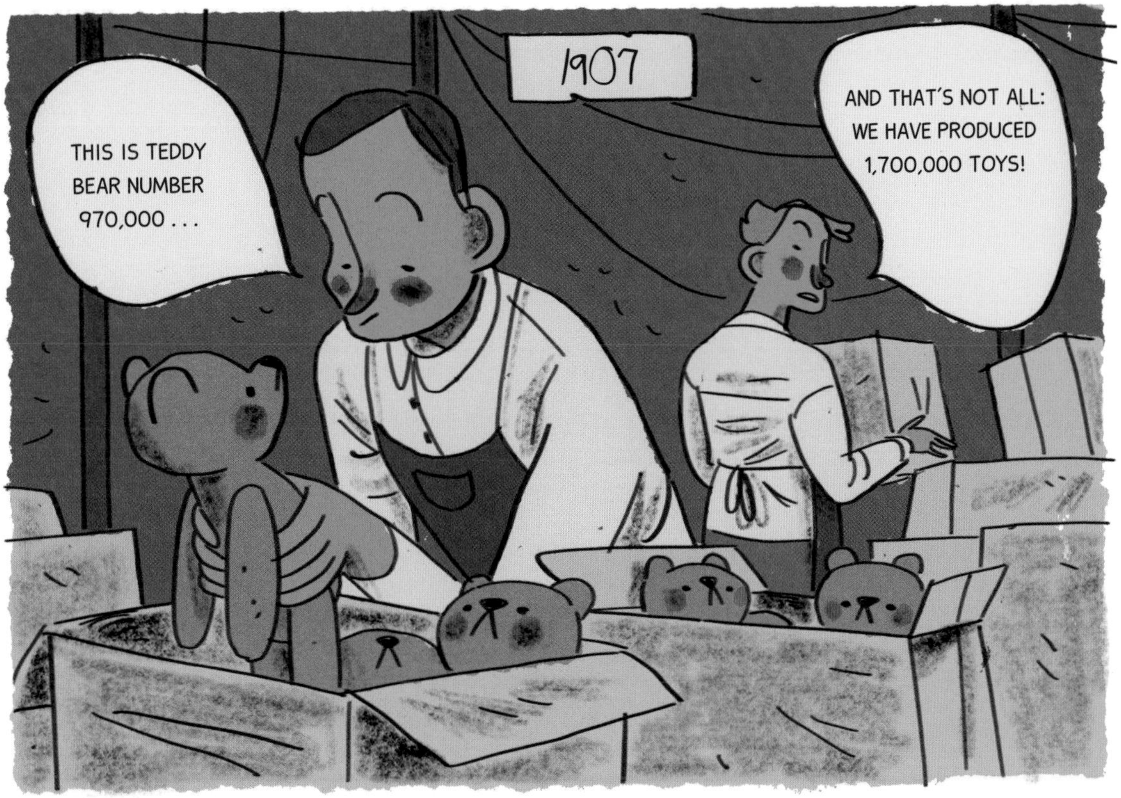
1907
THIS IS TEDDY BEAR NUMBER 970,000...
AND THAT'S NOT ALL: WE HAVE PRODUCED 1,700,000 TOYS!

Stephanie Louise Kwolek

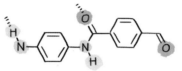

Stephanie Louise Kwolek never missed a thing, which is how she invented a superstrong material called Kevlar!

Stephanie Louise Kwolek was born in July 31, 1923, in Pittsburgh, Pennsylvania. As a child, she would play with fabrics because her mother was a seamstress, and she would dream of becoming a fashion designer. Growing up, however, Stephanie realized she wanted to help sick people, so she obtained a degree in chemistry. Soon after, she found a job in a chemical company to be able to pay for her medical studies. It was supposed to be a temporary position, but she liked the place a lot. She stayed there for over 40 years!

In fact, Kwolek discovered that she loved researching textile fibers and became one of the first women to work in industrial chemistry. She was a very thorough and extremely attentive person. Everyone knew that with her in the laboratory, everything was under control!

In 1964, during a laboratory experiment, Kwolek discovered a fiber that looked different from what she had expected. Simultaneously, the world needed a new material to build tires with.

Keep reading to see how Stephanie's invention changed the world!

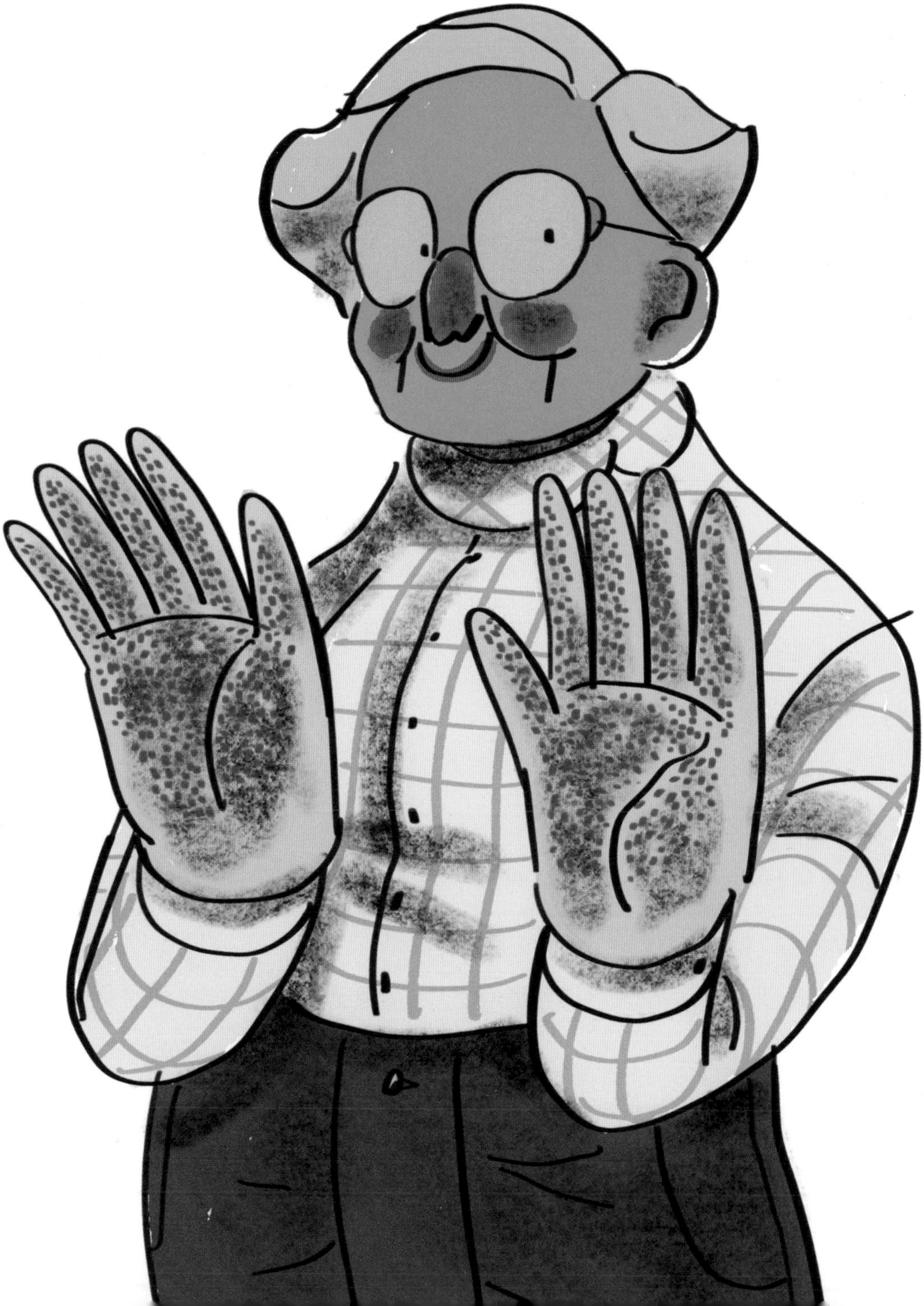

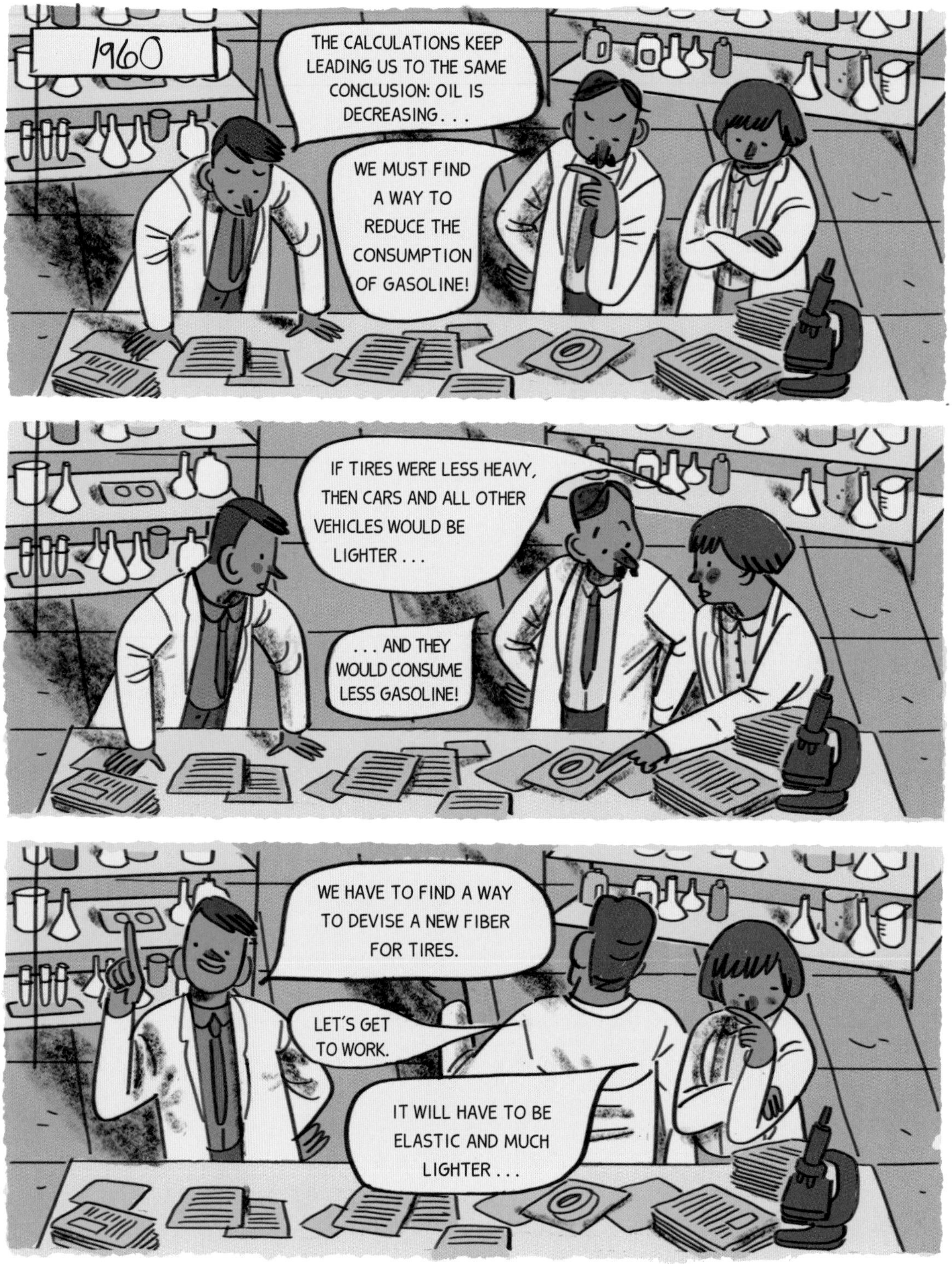
1960
THE CALCULATIONS KEEP LEADING US TO THE SAME CONCLUSION: OIL IS DECREASING. . .
WE MUST FIND A WAY TO REDUCE THE CONSUMPTION OF GASOLINE!
IF TIRES WERE LESS HEAVY, THEN CARS AND ALL OTHER VEHICLES WOULD BE LIGHTER . . .
. . . AND THEY WOULD CONSUME LESS GASOLINE!
WE HAVE TO FIND A WAY TO DEVISE A NEW FIBER FOR TIRES.
LET'S GET TO WORK.
IT WILL HAVE TO BE ELASTIC AND MUCH LIGHTER . . .

Stephanie thought she had the answer.

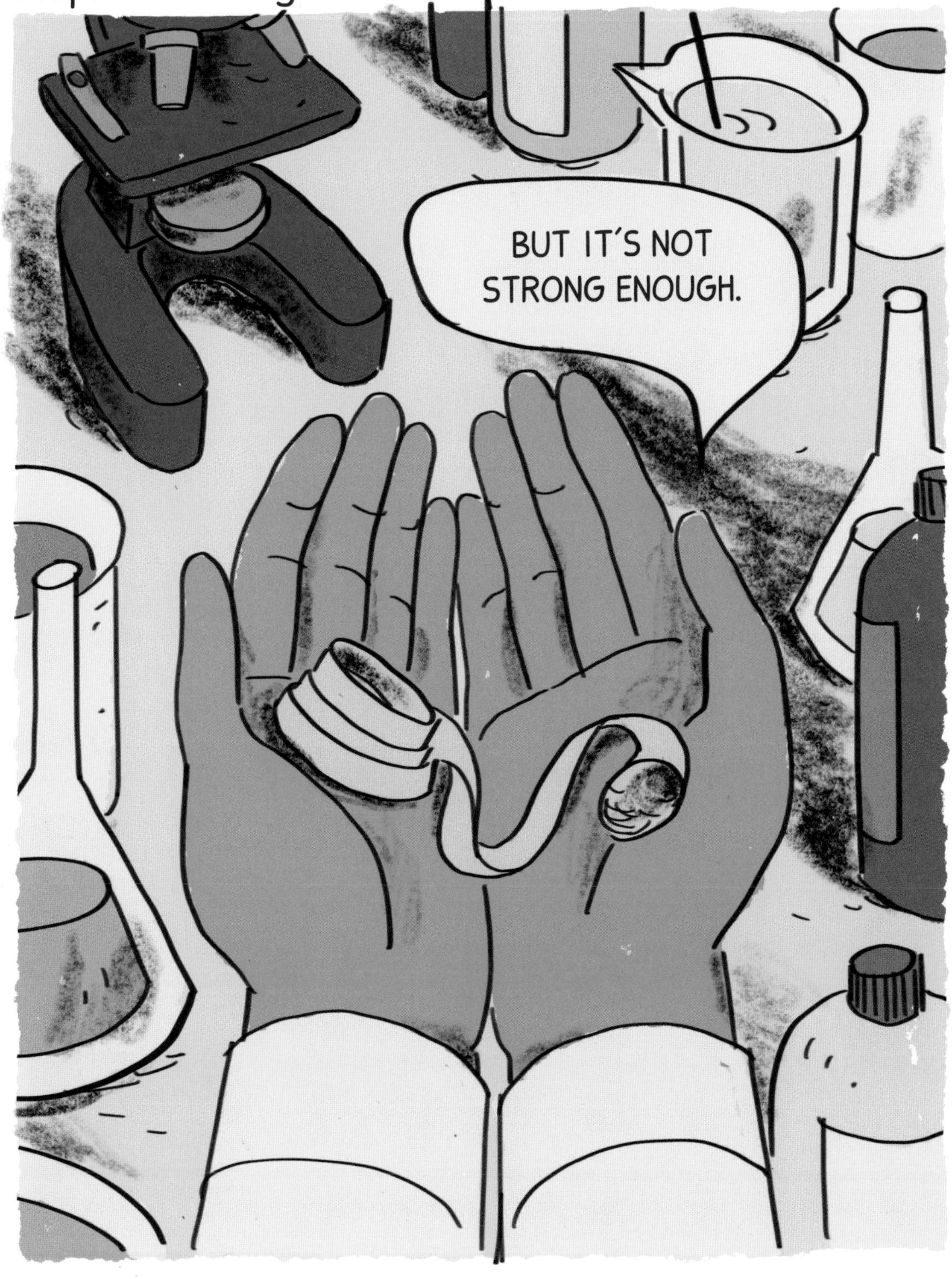
BUT IT'S NOT STRONG ENOUGH.

At first Stephanie feared that she had done something wrong!

Yet she had followed the correct procedure: She had taken fragments of fibers called polyamides and dissolved them in a liquid, then a machine (called a spinnerette) quickly rotated them to form a fiber.

However, the fiber that she eventually held in her hands was different from what she had expected. Stephanie didn't know what to think. She could have made a mistake. When experimenting in the lab it's very common for something to go wrong, as she knew.

Chemical Structure of Kevlar

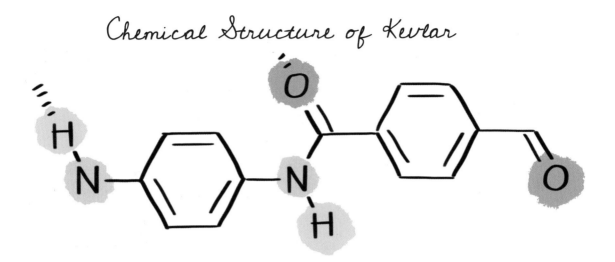

But she couldn't give up. She had to understand what had happened, without getting discouraged. She carried out numerous tests and repeated them until the results were confirmed. She didn't want to embarrass her research team: Everyone had worked hard with her, but she had to figure out what went wrong with the process . . . and in the end, she succeeded!

More importantly, she discovered that thanks to that mistake, she had created a much more resistant fiber: Kevlar.

At the time she had no idea how many ways this would be used in the future and how much it would improve the lives of people all over the world. Today, Kevlar is used in gloves, tires, and bulletproof vests, just to name a few. Thanks, Stephanie!

PERSEVERING IN UNDERSTANDING
A MISTAKE CAN LEAD TO NEW PATHS.

Stephanie Louise Kwolek   51

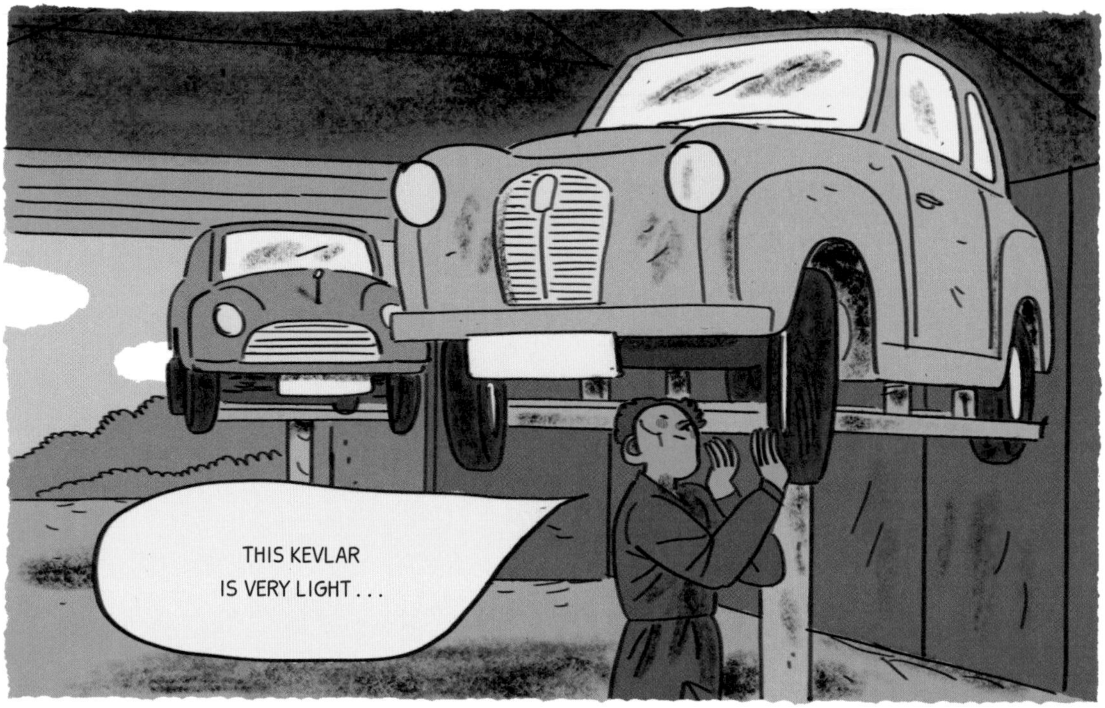
THIS KEVLAR IS VERY LIGHT . . .

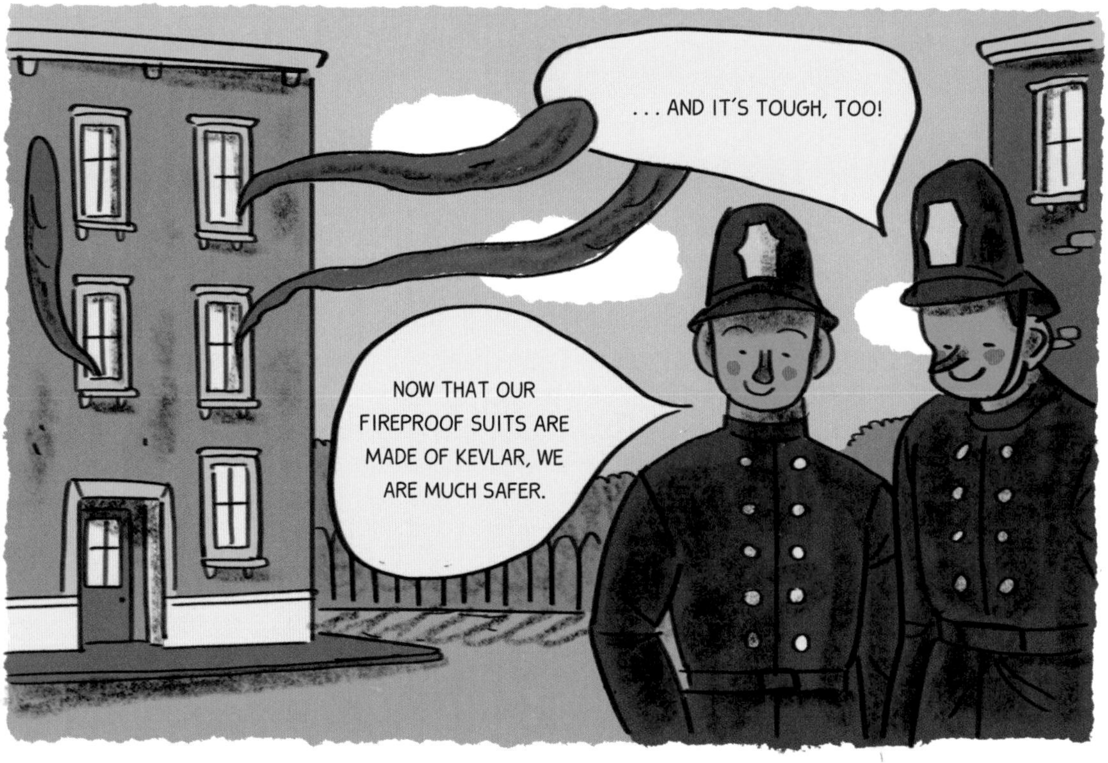
. . . AND IT'S TOUGH, TOO!
NOW THAT OUR FIREPROOF SUITS ARE MADE OF KEVLAR, WE ARE MUCH SAFER.

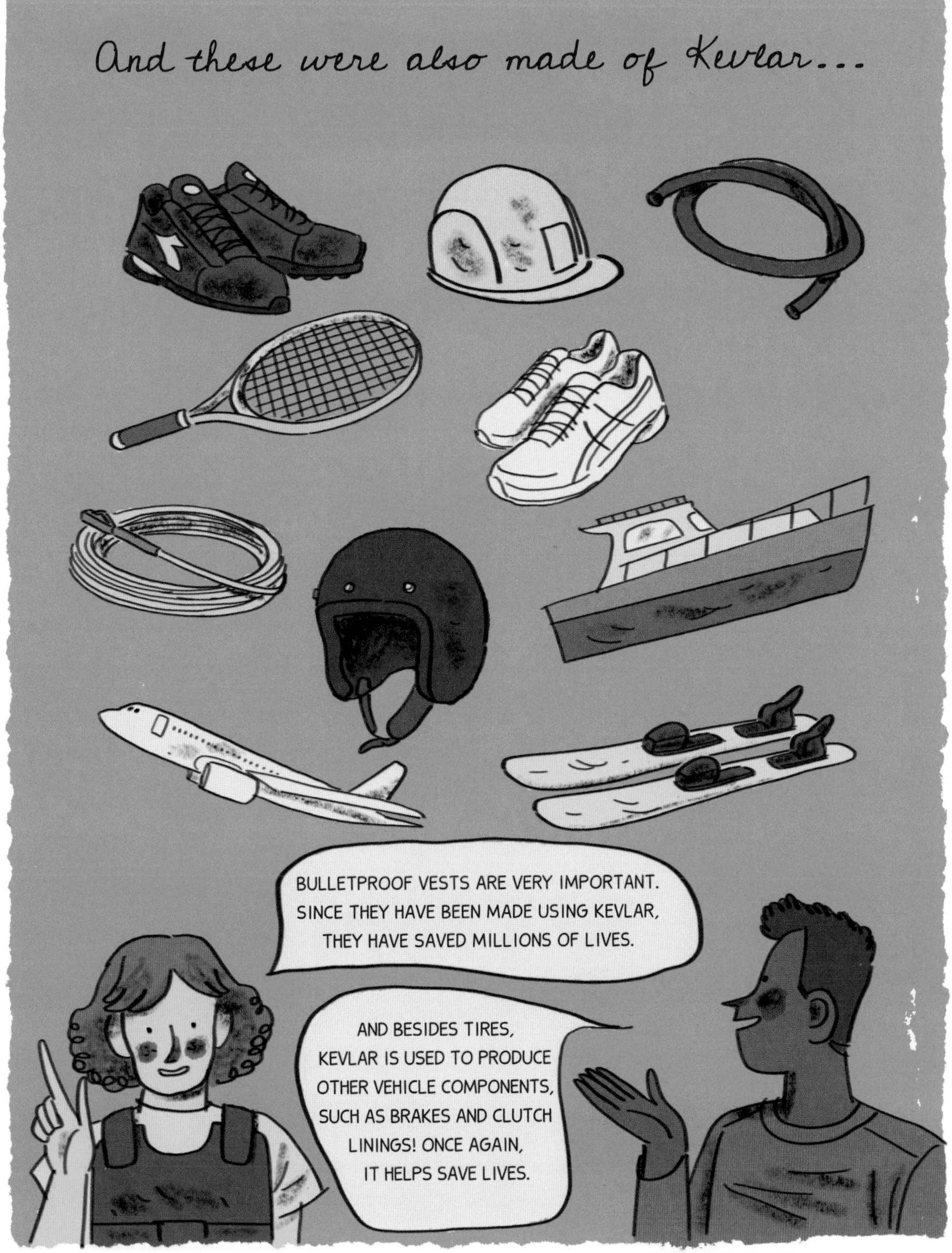
And these were also made of Kevlar...
BULLETPROOF VESTS ARE VERY IMPORTANT. SINCE THEY HAVE BEEN MADE USING KEVLAR, THEY HAVE SAVED MILLIONS OF LIVES.
AND BESIDES TIRES, KEVLAR IS USED TO PRODUCE OTHER VEHICLE COMPONENTS, SUCH AS BRAKES AND CLUTCH LININGS! ONCE AGAIN, IT HELPS SAVE LIVES.

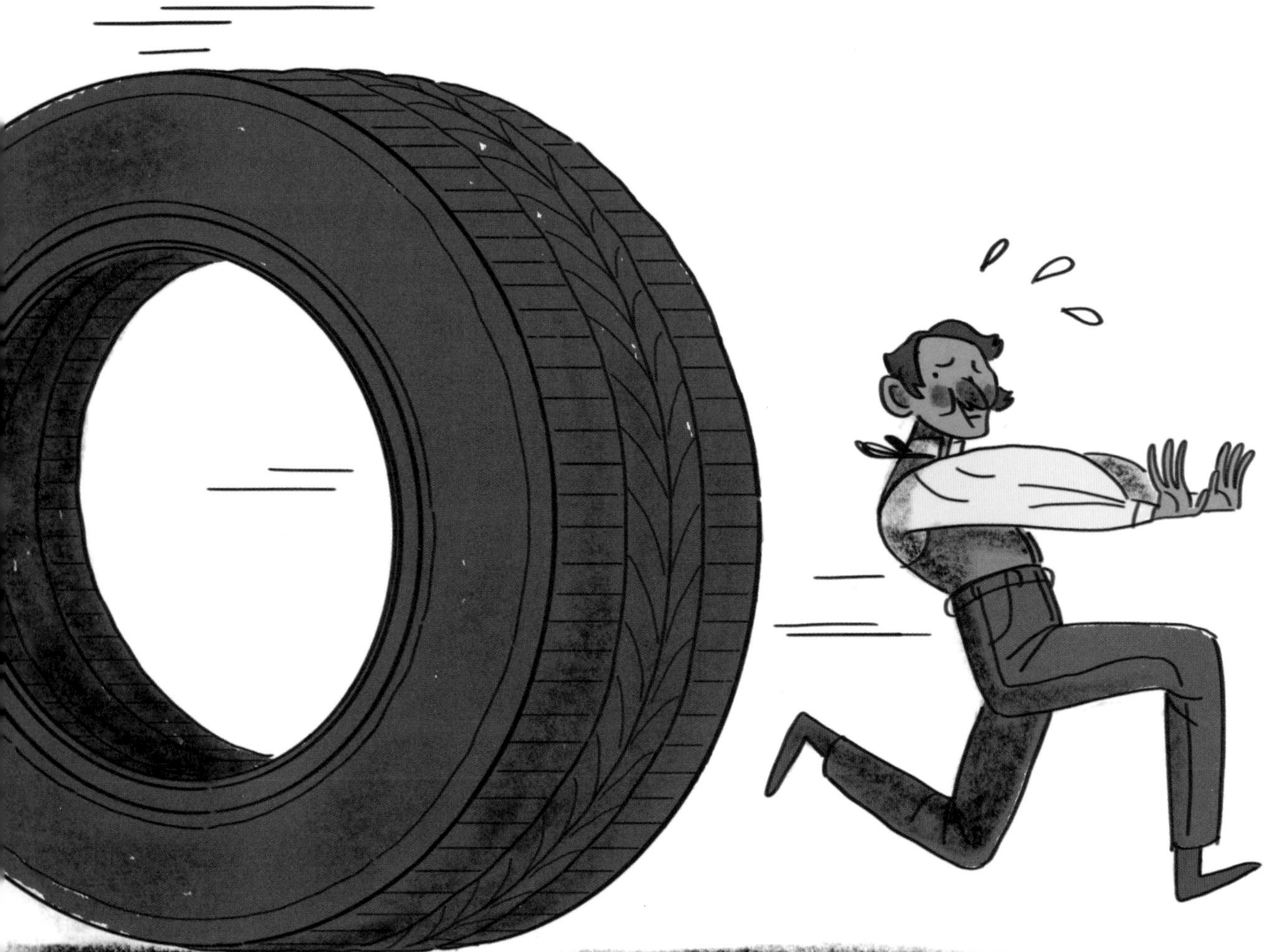

Charles Goodyear

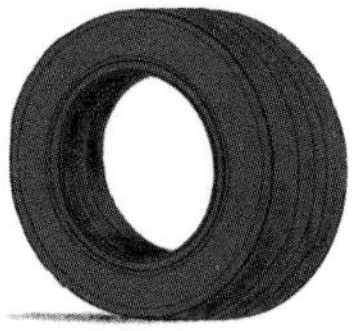

Charles Goodyear is known as the inventor of rubber.

Charles Goodyear was born on December 29, 1800, in New Haven, Connecticut. None of his early experiments succeeded—however, Charles had a dream: to discover the secrets of rubber. And he was determined to succeed!

For nearly 100 years, rubber had been extracted from the bark of some Brazilian plants. It was an elastic material that didn't last very long, plus it would become sticky at high temperatures and brittle at low ones. Goodyear was sure that it could be improved, and so he engaged in continuous experiments . . . thousands of them!

Then in 1839, one of his mixtures had an unexpected result: A compound made by pure chance proved to be decidedly more elastic than common rubber. Not only that, it was also resistant to heat and cold, and it was waterproof. Now it just needed to be put to use!

Turn the page to see how Goodyear's rubber came to be—
all thanks to his wife coming home one day!

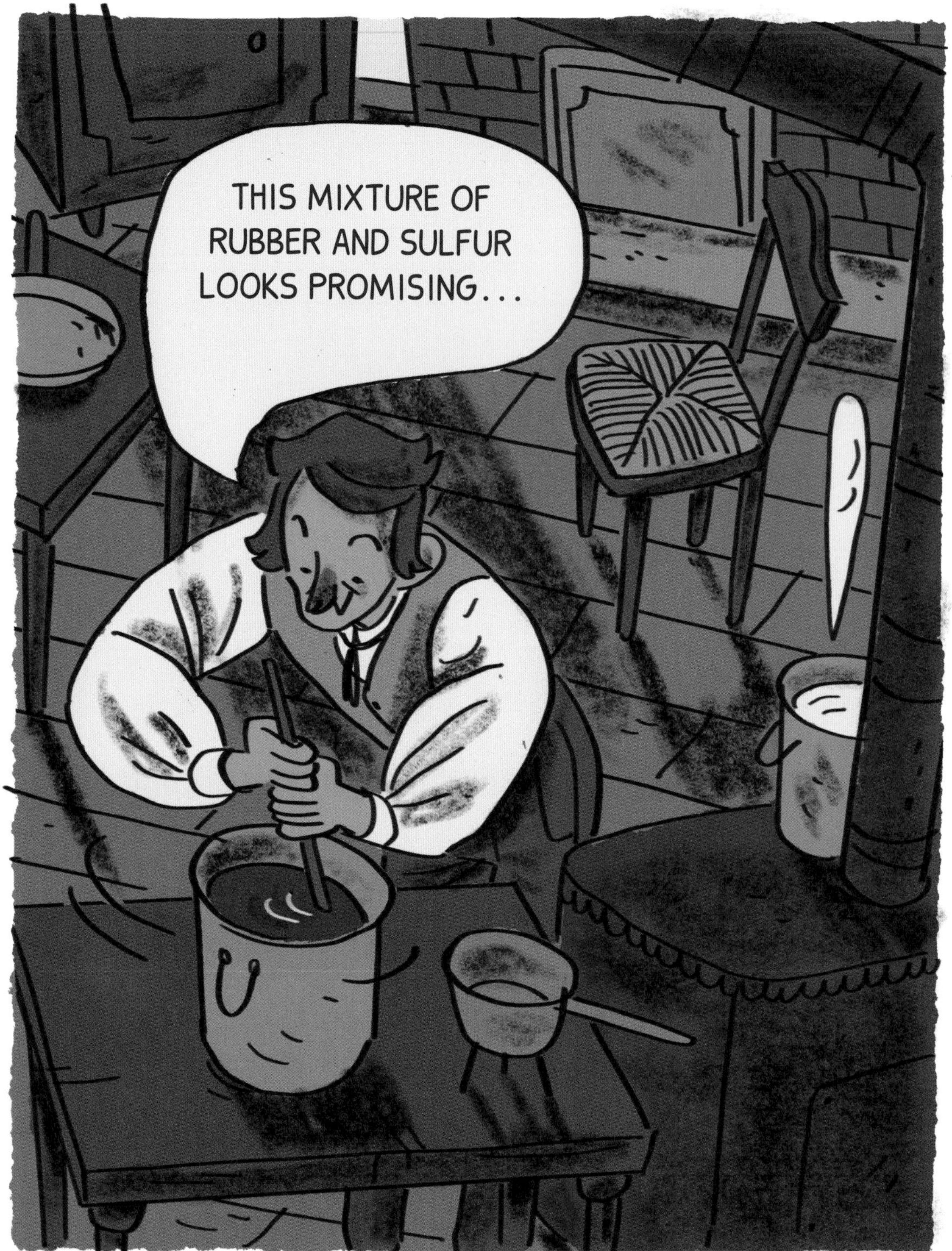
THIS MIXTURE OF RUBBER AND SULFUR LOOKS PROMISING...

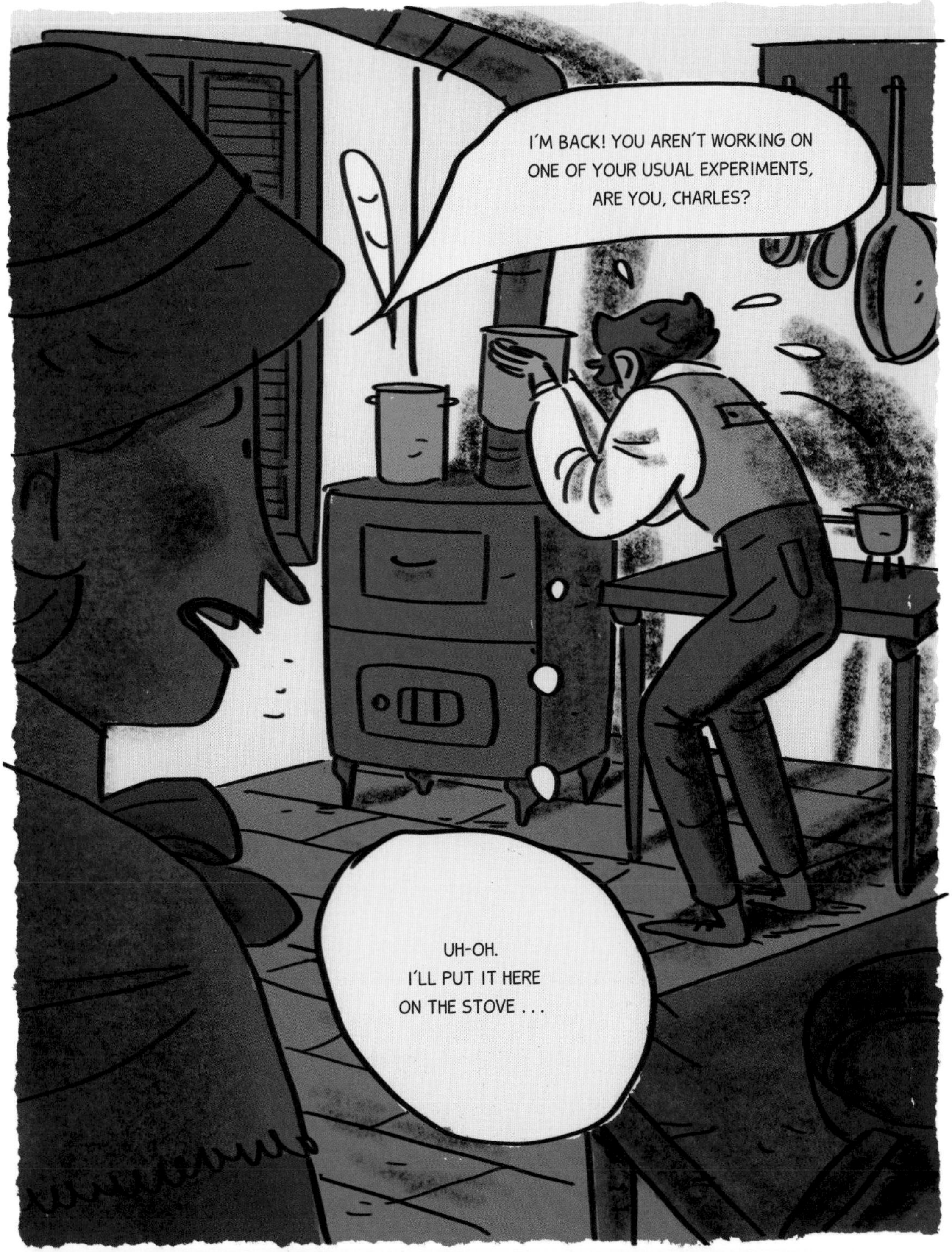
I'M BACK! YOU AREN'T WORKING ON ONE OF YOUR USUAL EXPERIMENTS, ARE YOU, CHARLES?
UH-OH. I'LL PUT IT HERE ON THE STOVE . . .

Nobody believed he could do it. The winter of 1839 was very harsh. Charles kept testing compounds to try to improve the rubber. He was so focused.

When his wife suddenly came home, Charles was caught off guard. His experiments would take a long time, preventing him from doing other jobs to help his family. This is why his wife, Clarissa, did not look favorably on them . . . not at all! It was for this reason that, when she entered the house, Charles instinctively placed the compound on which he was working on the burning stove along with other pots. "Maybe she won't notice it," he thought.

But soon after, a strange burning smell filled the kitchen. The mixture was getting too hot . . . it was about to catch fire!

He swiftly grabbed the pot and walked to the kitchen window, opened it, and tossed the mixture onto the fresh snow. Danger avoided! Too bad that he made a mistake in his experiment by putting the mixture first on the fire and then in the cold snow . . .

"Oh well," he said to himself, "I'll start over and this time I won't make mistakes."

But when he recovered what was left of the compound, he realized that something unexpected had happened: The high temperature had made the rubber even more elastic and, at the same time, also resistant to heat and cold. It was even waterproof!

Goodyear named this process "vulcanization" in honor of Vulcan, the Roman god of fire. And that was just the beginning: Vulcanized rubber is still being produced today, almost 200 years later! Although, we don't recommend using a stove without an adult's supervision.

PERSEVERING ON INTUITION WITH A VISION OF THE FUTURE CAN TAKE
YOU A LONG WAY, EVEN IF MANY MISTAKES ARE REQUIRED.

Charles Goodyear

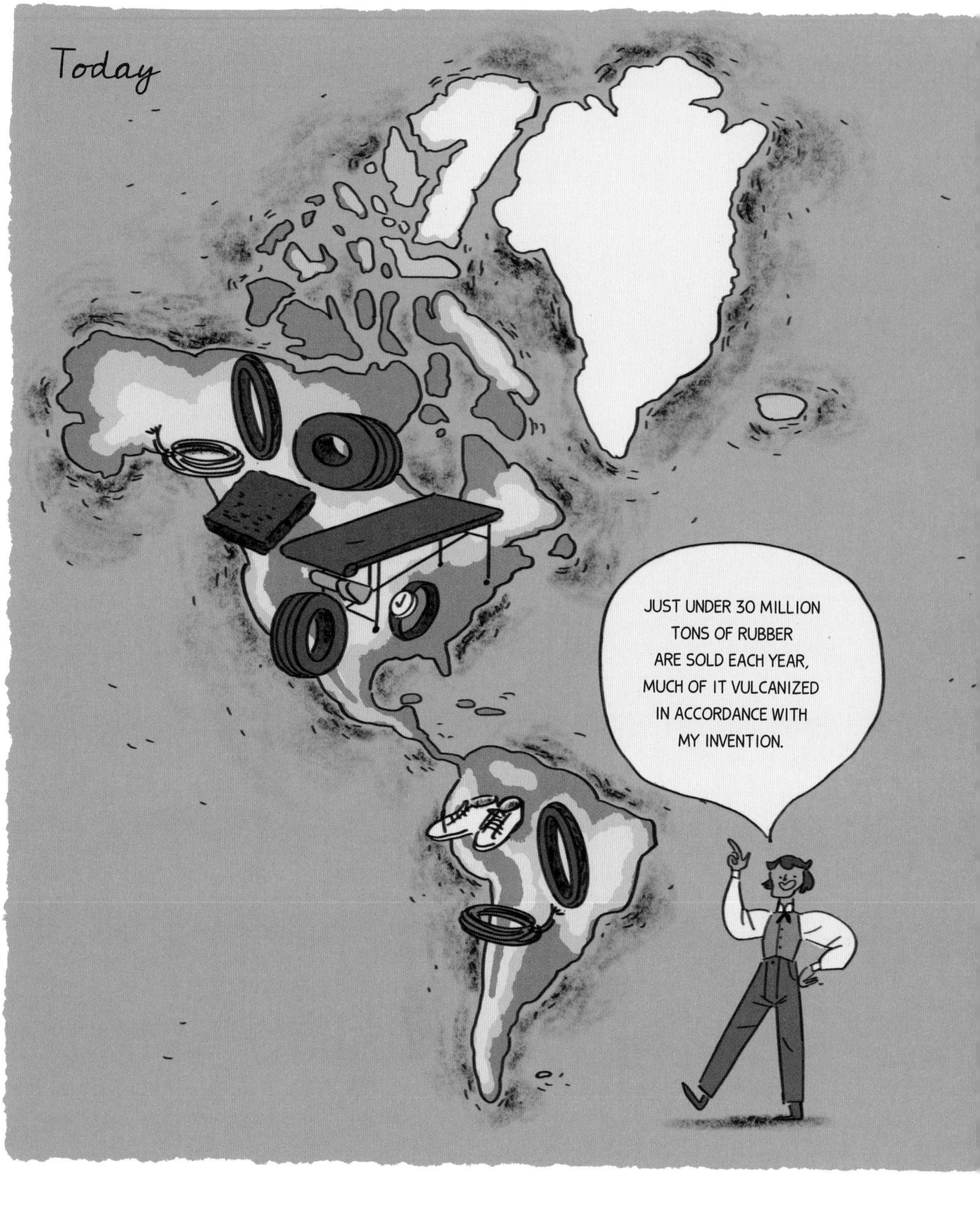
Today
JUST UNDER 30 MILLION TONS OF RUBBER ARE SOLD EACH YEAR, MUCH OF IT VULCANIZED IN ACCORDANCE WITH MY INVENTION.

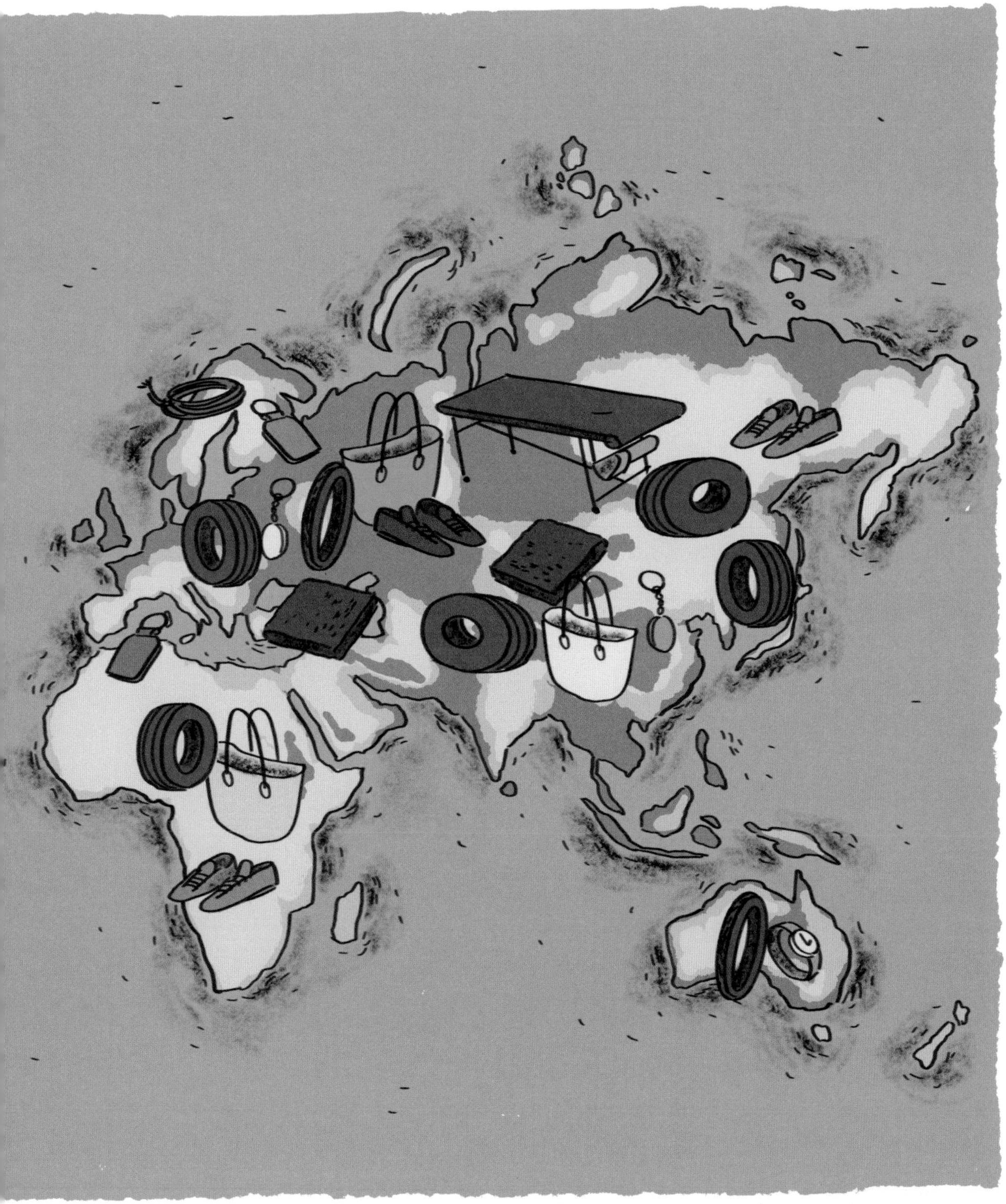

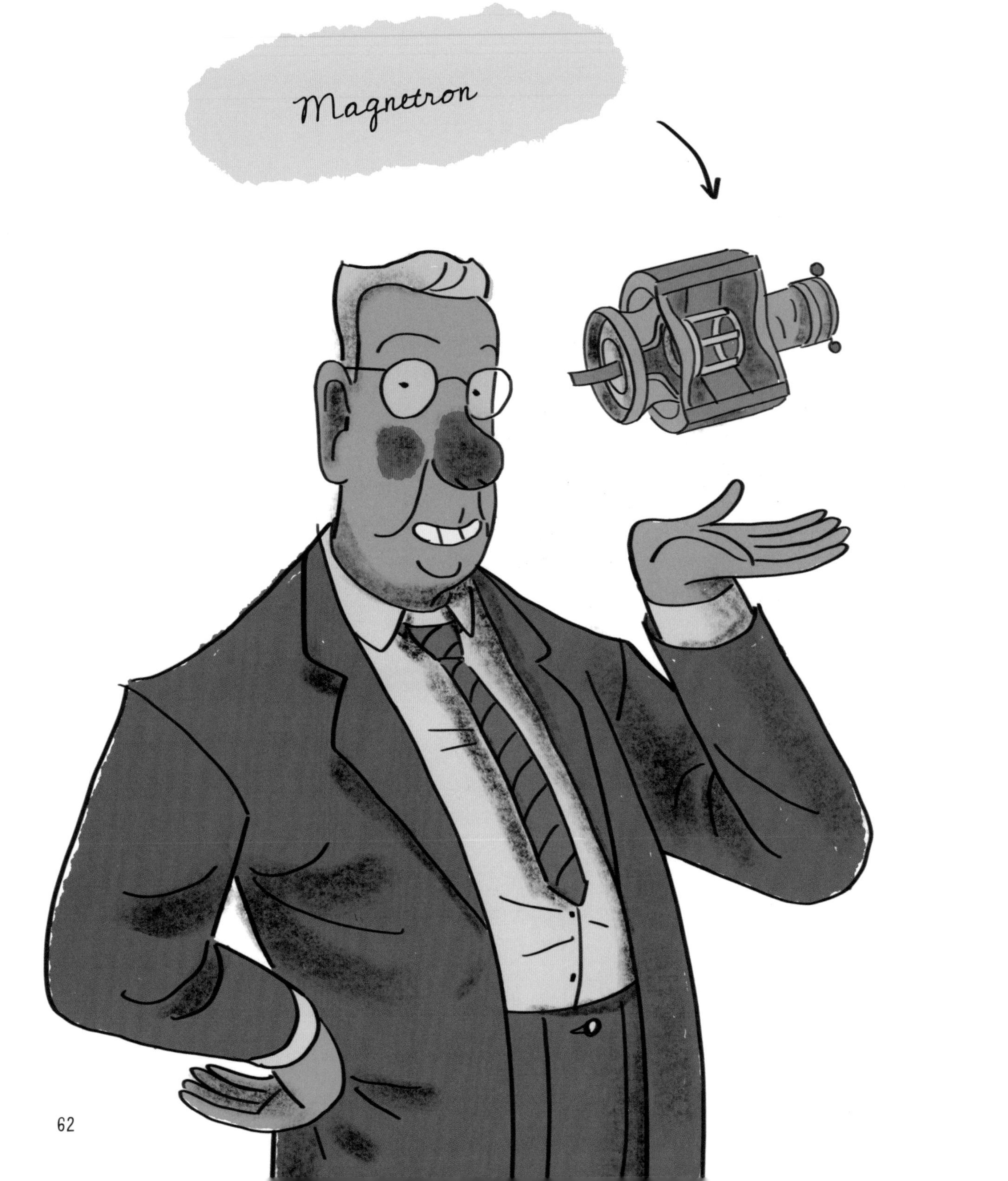
Magnetron

Percy Spencer

Percy Spencer was fascinated by the "why" of things.

Percy Spencer was born on July 19, 1894, in Howland, Maine. From an early age, Percy was very curious. He loved discovering how and why things worked. Left without parents as a child, he traveled with his aunt, who lived off temporary jobs. Thanks to this, he learned to work his way up and how to do things on his own. He didn't finish school because he went to work, installing electricity on construction sites.

Since Percy knew nothing about electricity, he studied at night and learned by practice until he became a skilled electrician. But Percy's life changed when he learned about the *Titanic* tragedy and how the wireless telegraph had saved the survivors. He enlisted in the navy to become a radio operator on ships. Again, Spencer had to study and learn on his own. And he succeeded! Hooray!

Discharged at the end of the First World War, he joined a company that worked with the Department of Defense. Percy was delighted! He could work with physicists, engineers, inventors . . . but he always used his practical approach to the "why" of things. He helped develop technologies and components until his intuition led to a major change in food preparation: the microwave oven!

Turn the page to learn how Percy invented the microwave oven!

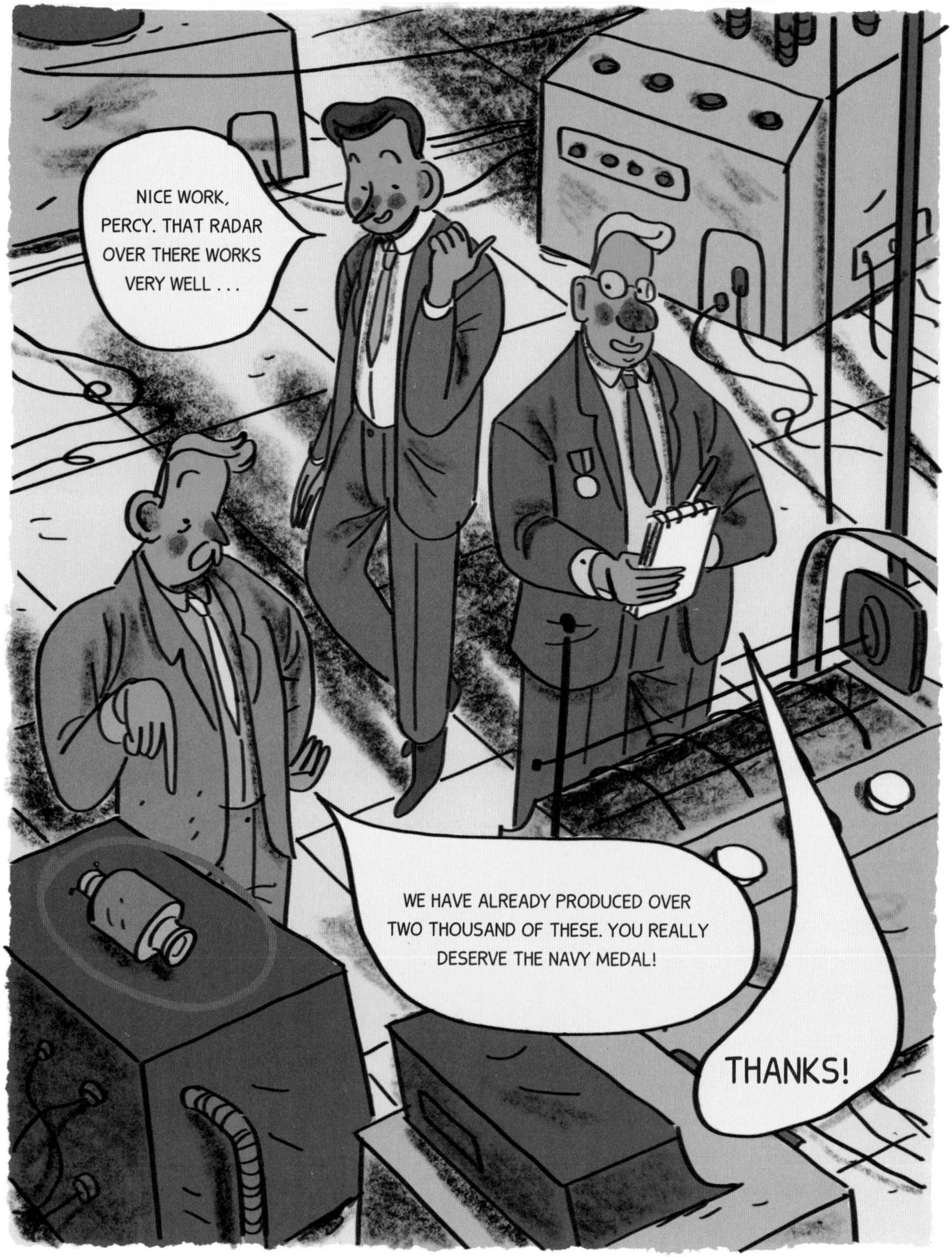
NICE WORK, PERCY. THAT RADAR OVER THERE WORKS VERY WELL . . .
WE HAVE ALREADY PRODUCED OVER TWO THOUSAND OF THESE. YOU REALLY DESERVE THE NAVY MEDAL!
THANKS!

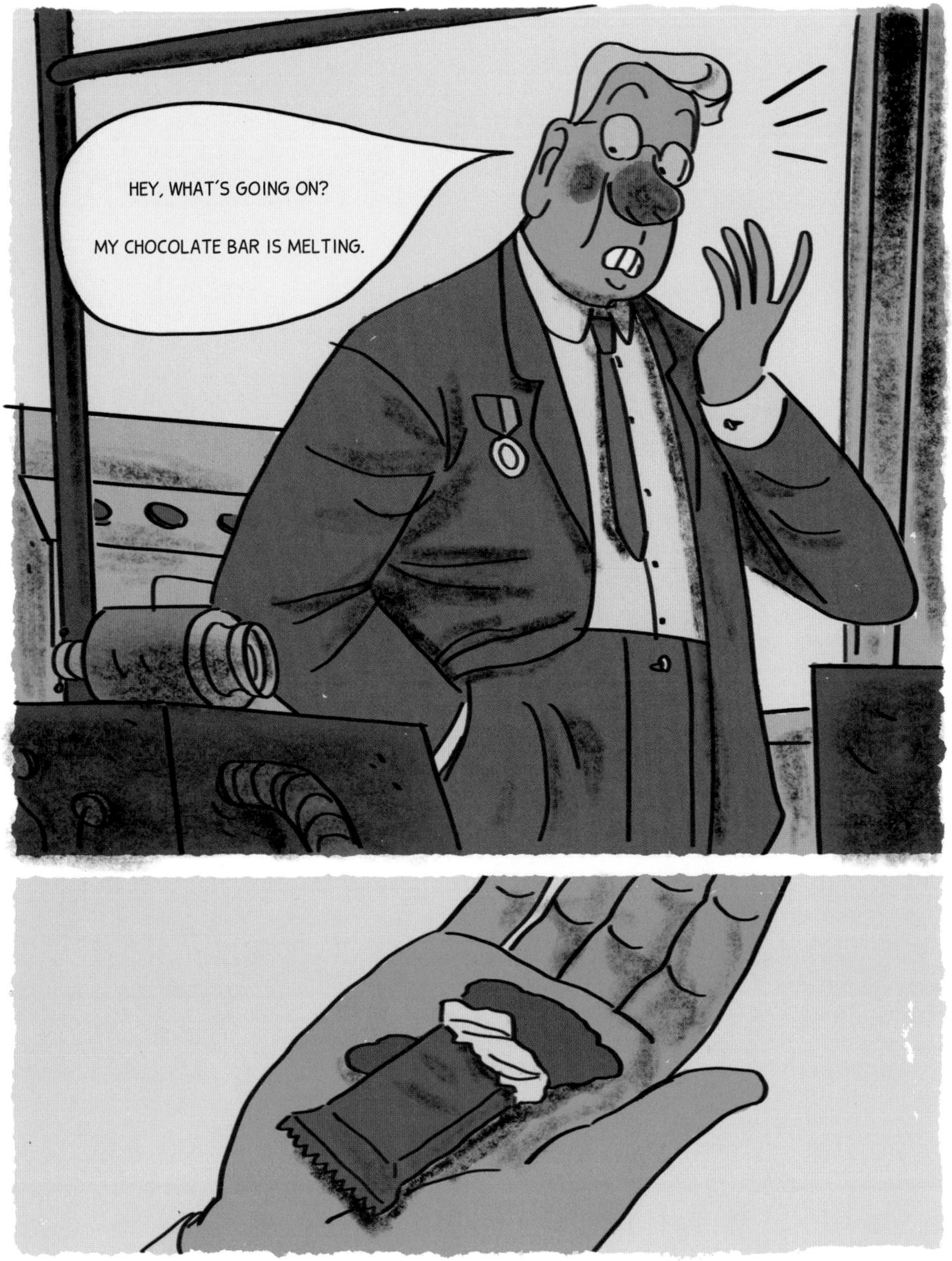
HEY, WHAT'S GOING ON?
MY CHOCOLATE BAR IS MELTING.

"The scientist knows that many things will not work.
Percy Spencer doesn't know what can't be done,"
wrote *Reader's Digest.*

Percy discovered that the chocolate bar in his pocket was melting just because he stood near the radar equipment, which blew him away. It was a mistake, of course—that his snack had melted and now he would be left with an empty stomach. Yet he wanted to know why it had happened!

"What if the energy of the radio waves could also heat other food quickly?" he wondered.

SPLAT!

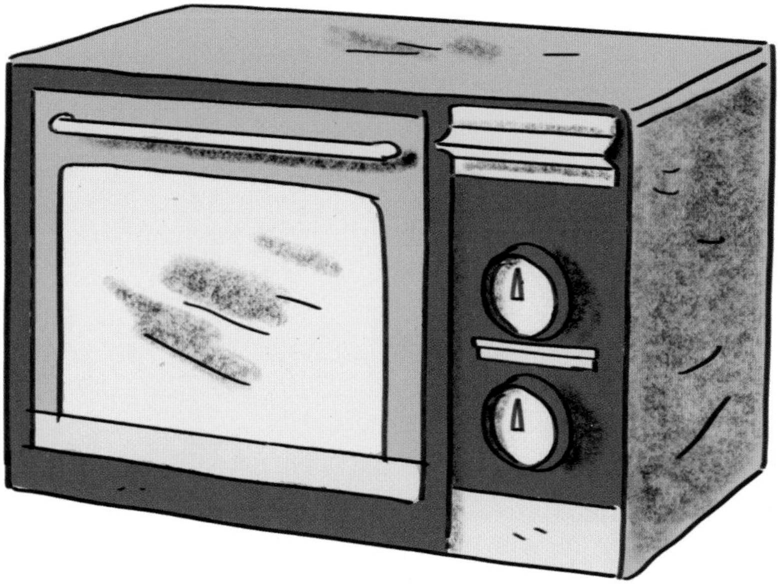

It didn't quite look like this yet, though.

Percy immediately gave it a try: He put a bowl full of popcorn kernels near the tube with the radar and . . . *Pop! Pop!* In no time, the bowl was filled with crackling, hot popcorn!

Then Percy conducted another test: He put a teapot, with an egg inside, under the radar tubes, and just as a colleague approached, the cooked egg exploded in his face!

After many attempts, Percy managed to put the device inside a closed metal box. In this way the waves remained in the box, heating only the inside. He had just invented the microwave oven!

SOMETIMES WHAT HAPPENS AROUND US IS RANDOM, AND YET, PERSISTING ON INTUITION, DESPITE MISTAKES, BRINGS NEW RESULTS.

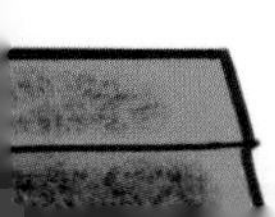

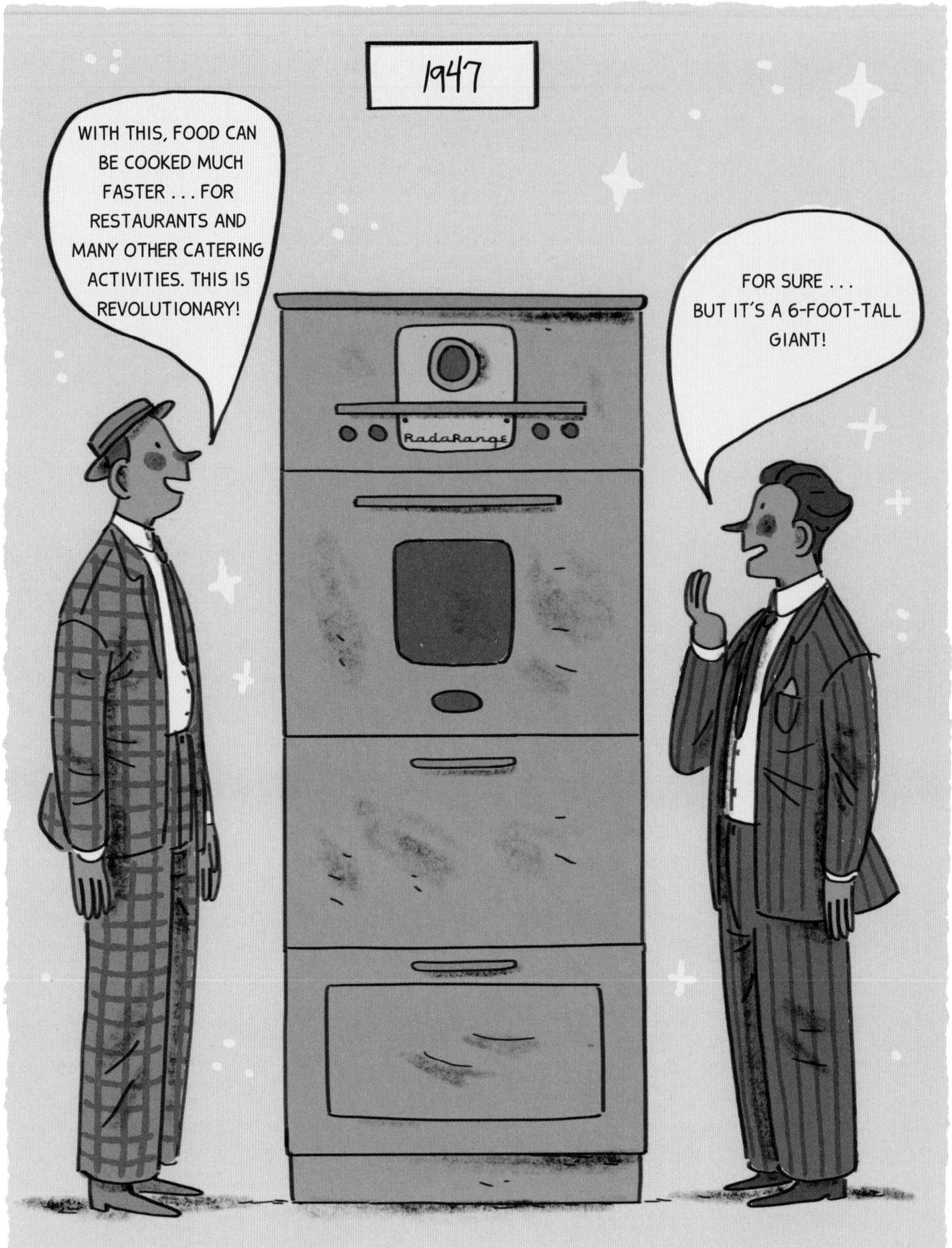
1947
WITH THIS, FOOD CAN BE COOKED MUCH FASTER . . . FOR RESTAURANTS AND MANY OTHER CATERING ACTIVITIES. THIS IS REVOLUTIONARY!
RadaRange
FOR SURE . . . BUT IT'S A 6-FOOT-TALL GIANT!

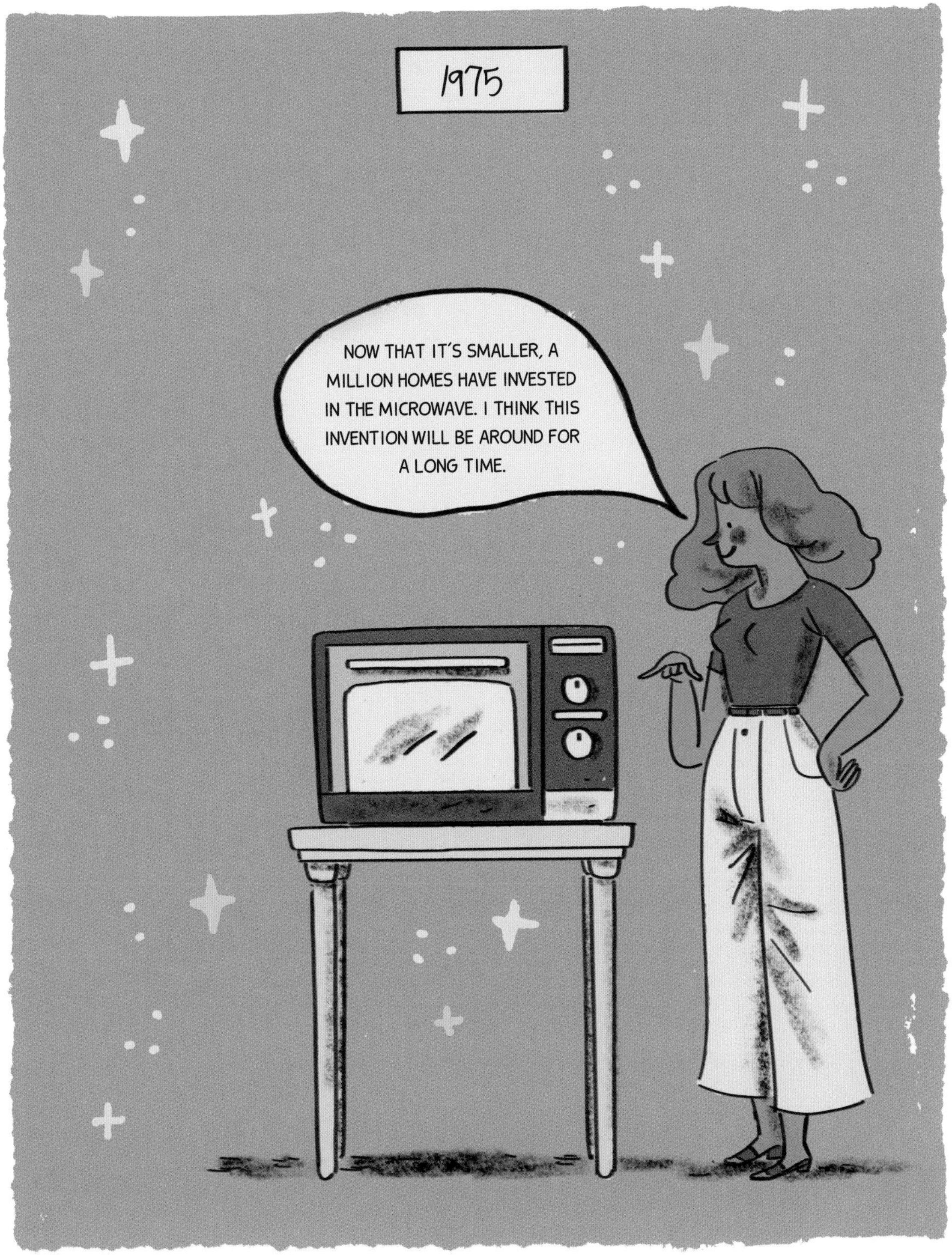
1975
NOW THAT IT'S SMALLER, A MILLION HOMES HAVE INVESTED IN THE MICROWAVE. I THINK THIS INVENTION WILL BE AROUND FOR A LONG TIME.

John Stith Pemberton

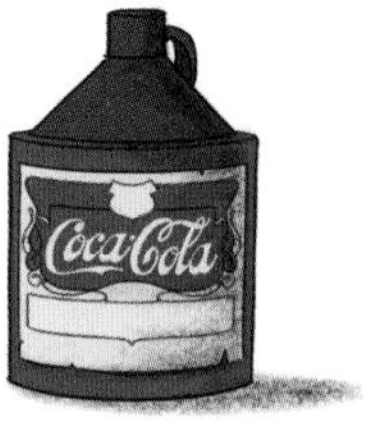
Coca-Cola

John Stith Pemberton had no doubts:
Medical remedies were his passion.

John Stith Pemberton was born on July 8, 1831, in Knoxville, Georgia, and studied medicine and pharmacology. He learned to make herbal preparations to cure ailments, even if at the time, many did not want to try them. At the age of 24, Pemberton founded a unique pharmaceutical company with some partners. They produced medical preparations that were useful for treating various ailments . . . and they worked!

Unfortunately, the American Civil War broke out shortly after, and he enlisted.

In 1865, during a battle, John was wounded in the chest and was treated with medicine. The more medicine he took, the more he wanted . . . and he didn't like that effect at all. Back home, he began to study the medicine that doctors had given him, hoping to improve it. Eventually, he came up with a recipe with some healing plants and wine. He began selling it as a pain reliever while his pharmaceutical company grew.

Things were going just fine!

However, in 1886, a new law prohibited the consumption of alcohol, which was an ingredient in his concoction, so he needed a nonalcoholic remedy! During that hot and humid summer, he went back to work . . .

Keep reading to discover how John invented Coca-Cola!

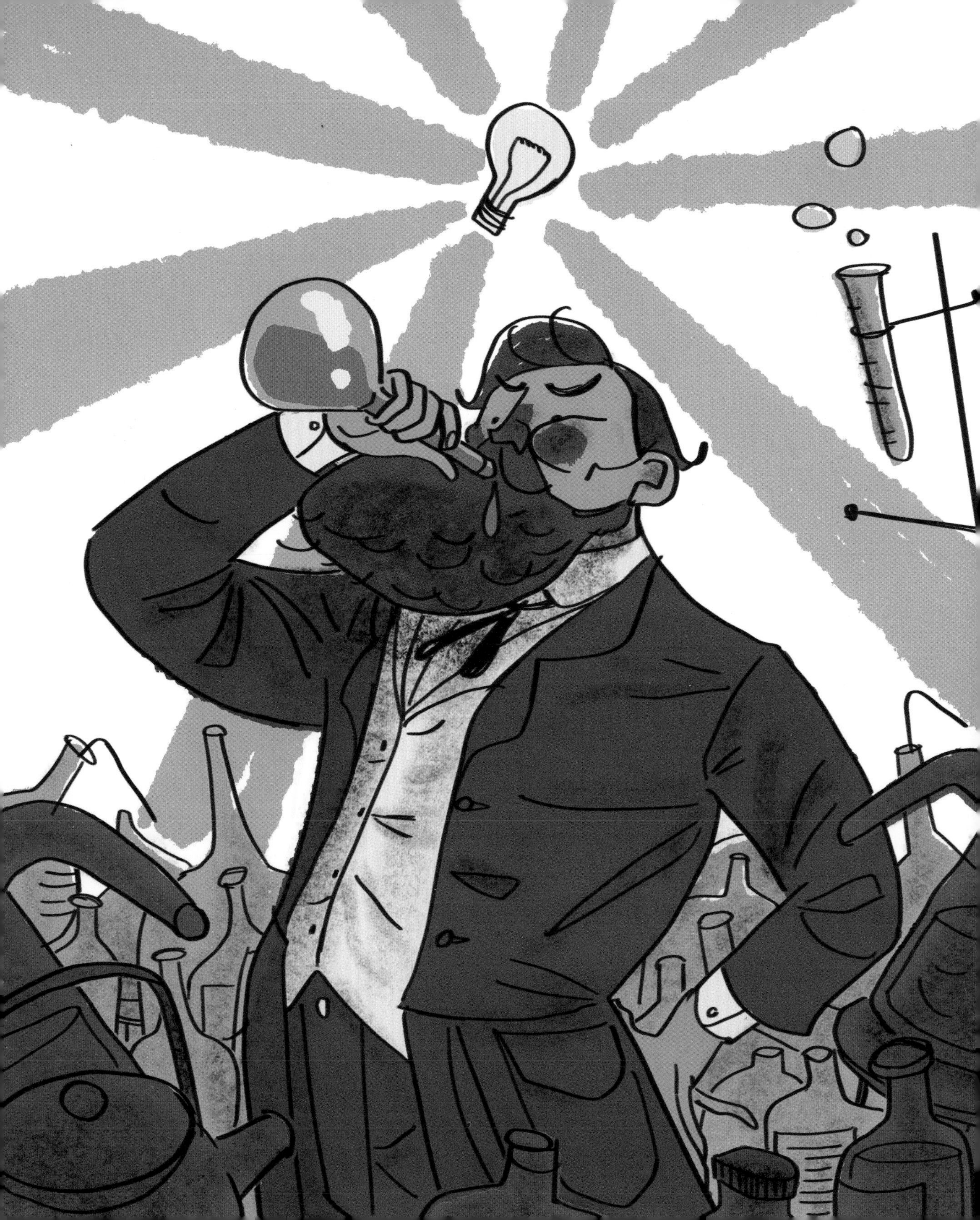

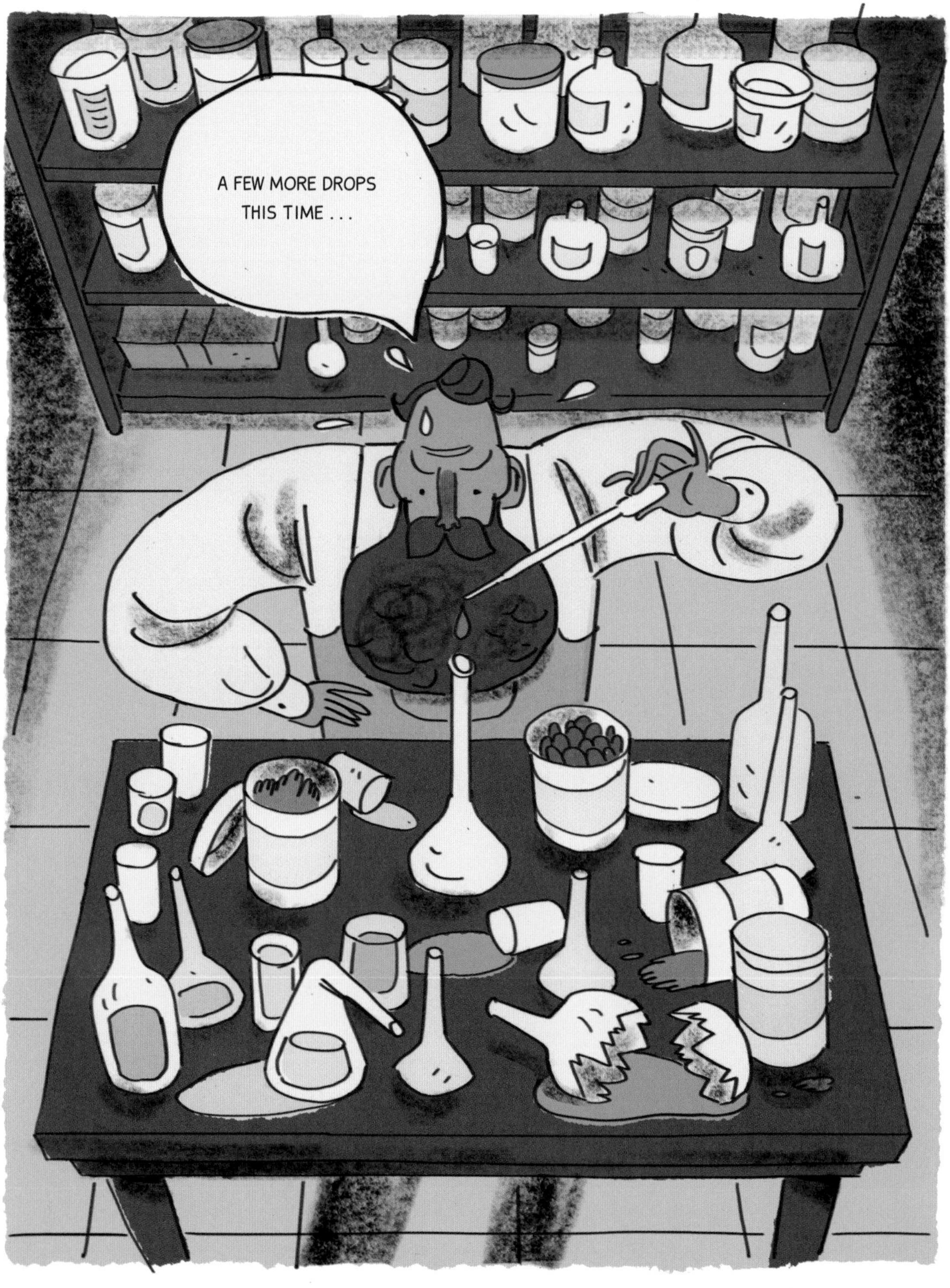
A FEW MORE DROPS THIS TIME . . .

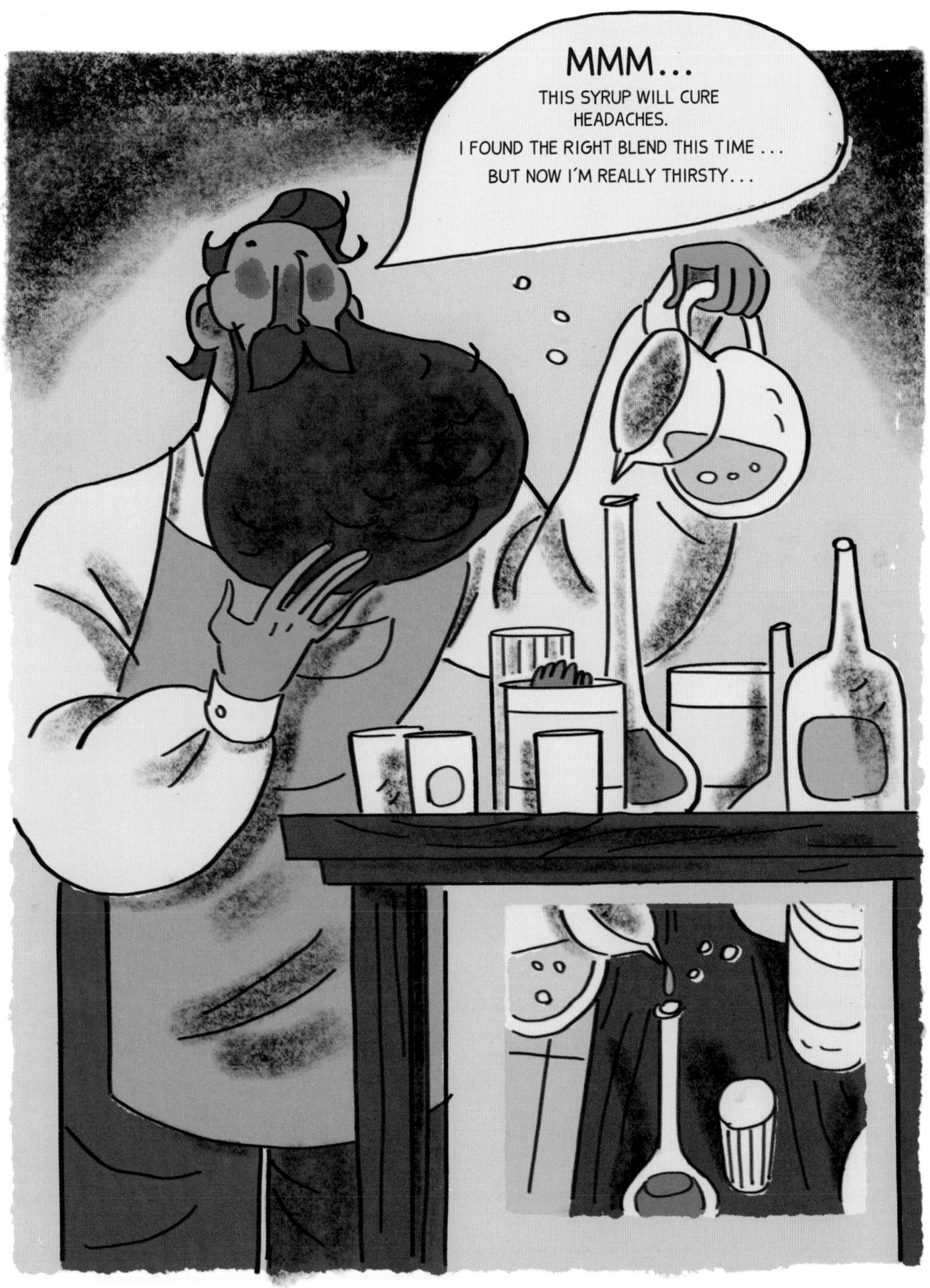
MMM...
THIS SYRUP WILL CURE HEADACHES.
I FOUND THE RIGHT BLEND THIS TIME . . .
BUT NOW I'M REALLY THIRSTY. . .

When making a new discovery, it's easy to get carried away.

While looking at the tonic he had just created, John accidentally poured in sparkling water.

"Now I'll have to redo the mixture," he thought, checking the recipe.

He raised the glass to his lips, out of pure curiosity, and tasted it. His eyes widened. It was nice! He drank more . . . it wasn't bad at all! Then he filled a jug and took it to a nearby pharmacy.

"Delicious and thirst-quenching!" the owners said, sipping it and offering to sell it as a takeout drink.

That day, May 8, 1886, the new tonic started to be sold in pharmacies. John was over the moon! When he explained his invention, his friend and partner Frank Mason Robinson was thrilled.

MIX
MIX

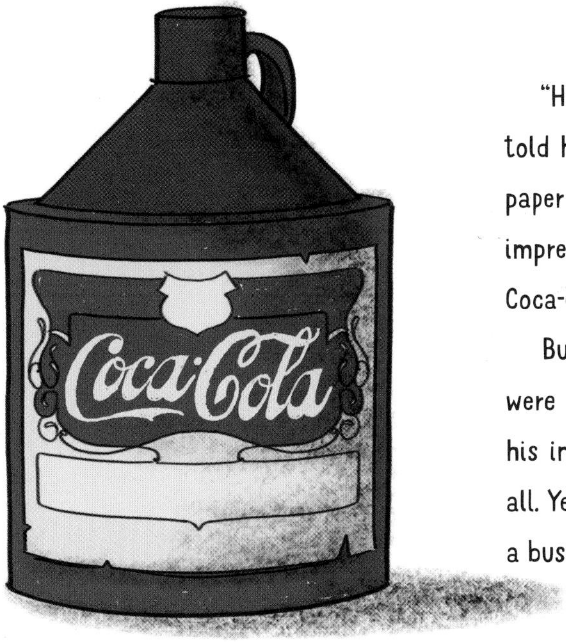
Coca-Cola

"How about calling it Coca-Cola?" he told him. He wrote the name on a sheet of paper in cursive handwriting. Everyone was impressed. After all these years, it is still the Coca-Cola logo.

But the first year, only nine glasses a day were sold. John was disappointed. Perhaps his invention was not such a success after all. Yet someone did not agree: Asa Candler, a businessman.

Candler's plan was to sell Coca-Cola in all shops and supermarkets as an exquisite, refreshing, invigorating, stimulating drink (as one could read in advertisements). In a few years it became very popular!

SOMETIMES WHAT SEEMS
BADLY DONE JUST
NEEDS
A NEW PATH.

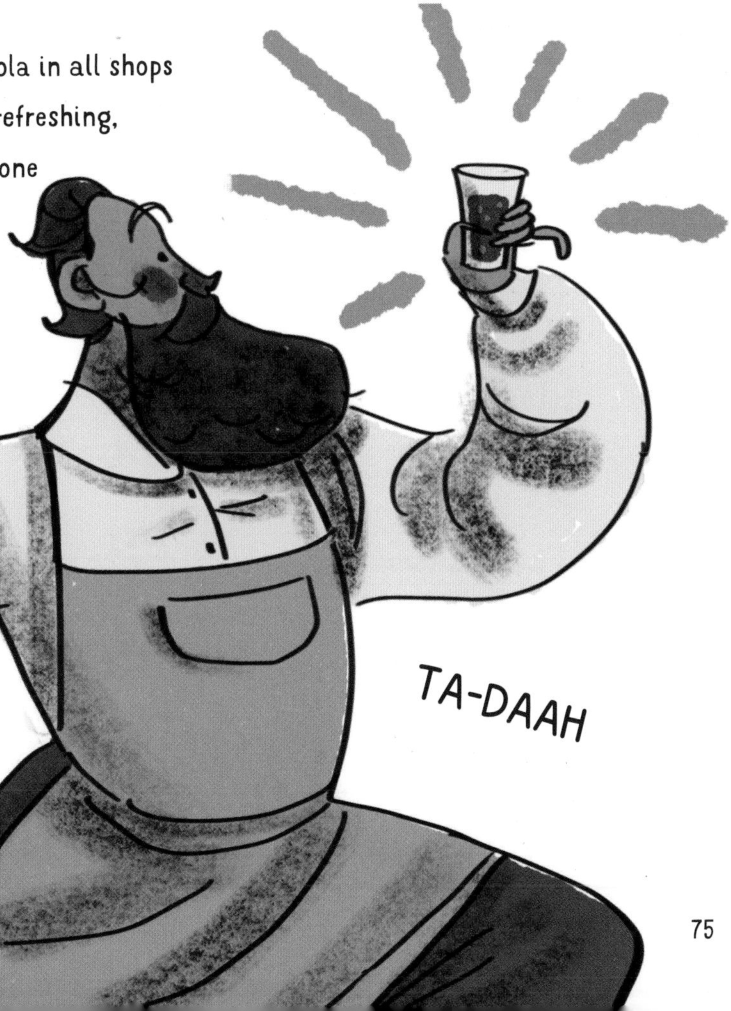
TA-DAAH

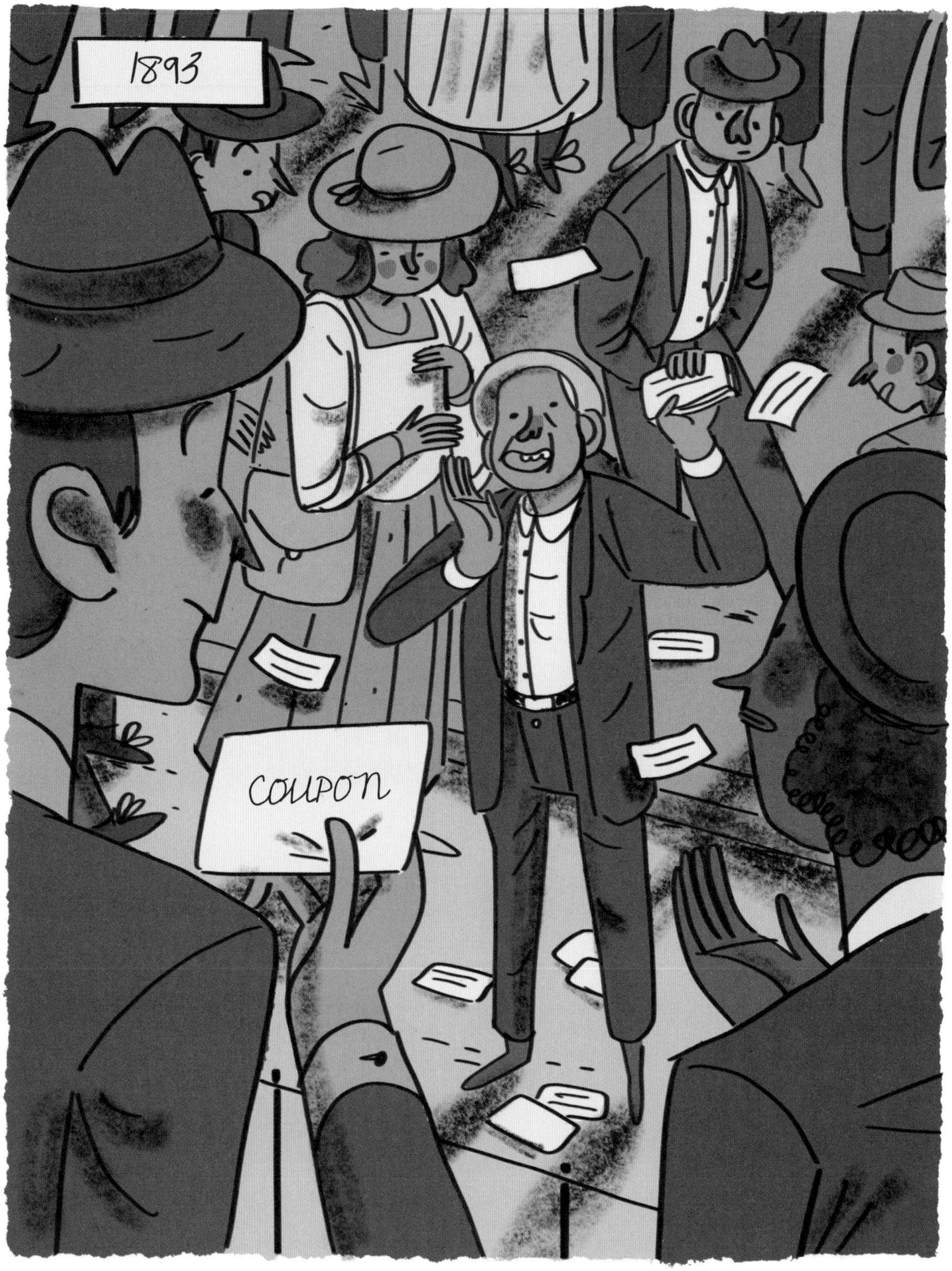
1893
COUPON

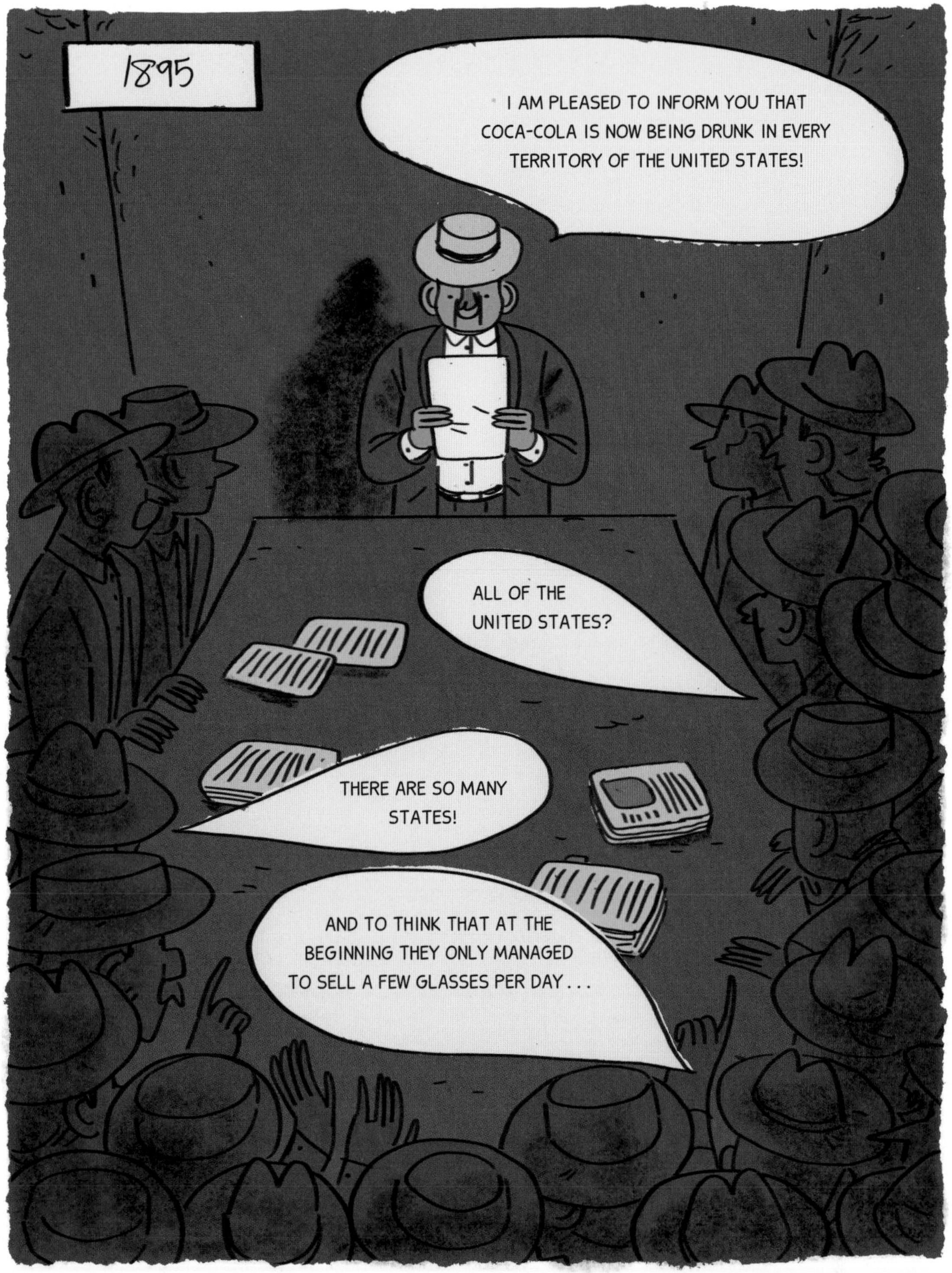
1895
I AM PLEASED TO INFORM YOU THAT COCA-COLA IS NOW BEING DRUNK IN EVERY TERRITORY OF THE UNITED STATES!
ALL OF THE UNITED STATES?
THERE ARE SO MANY STATES!
AND TO THINK THAT AT THE BEGINNING THEY ONLY MANAGED TO SELL A FEW GLASSES PER DAY . . .

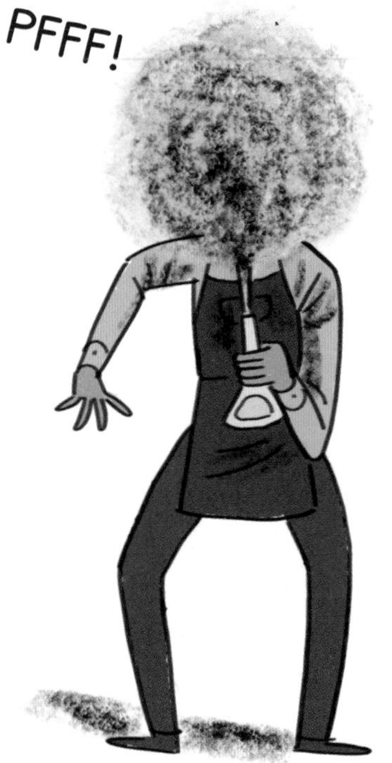
PFFF!

SO NOW, HERE WE ARE,
AT THE END OF THE BOOK . . .

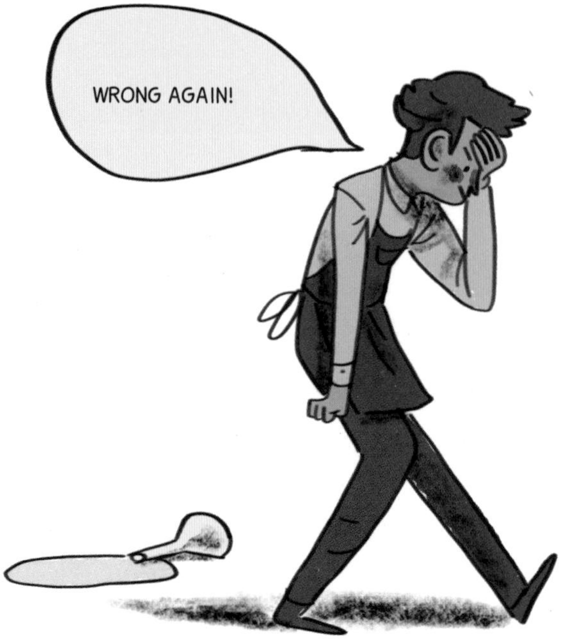
WRONG AGAIN!

You just read 10 very different stories. Scientists, pharmacists, workers, seamstresses, engineers . . . now you know what their secret is, don't you?

MAKING MISTAKES!

Every one of them made many mistakes before discovering or inventing something that changed the lives of many people.

And those mistakes were often so different from one another. Sometimes an attempt seemed wrong. Other times so many attempts were made the inventor lost count. Or it was an unexpected event that triggered the error . . .

Nobody likes to make mistakes. Yet that's exactly what happened to the 10 talents in this book. **THEY MADE MISTAKES AND DID NOT REGRET THEM.** On the contrary, they tried to understand and made an effort to learn from them. Some tried and tried again because they didn't know exactly how to create the idea they had in mind.

Others weren't even sure if they had really discovered something! It took a lot of patience and work, without getting discouraged, because every mistake brought them closer to discovery.

You've just read 10 examples of how **BEING WRONG CAN GET ANYONE VERY, VERY FAR . . .**

So, now, what are you waiting for?

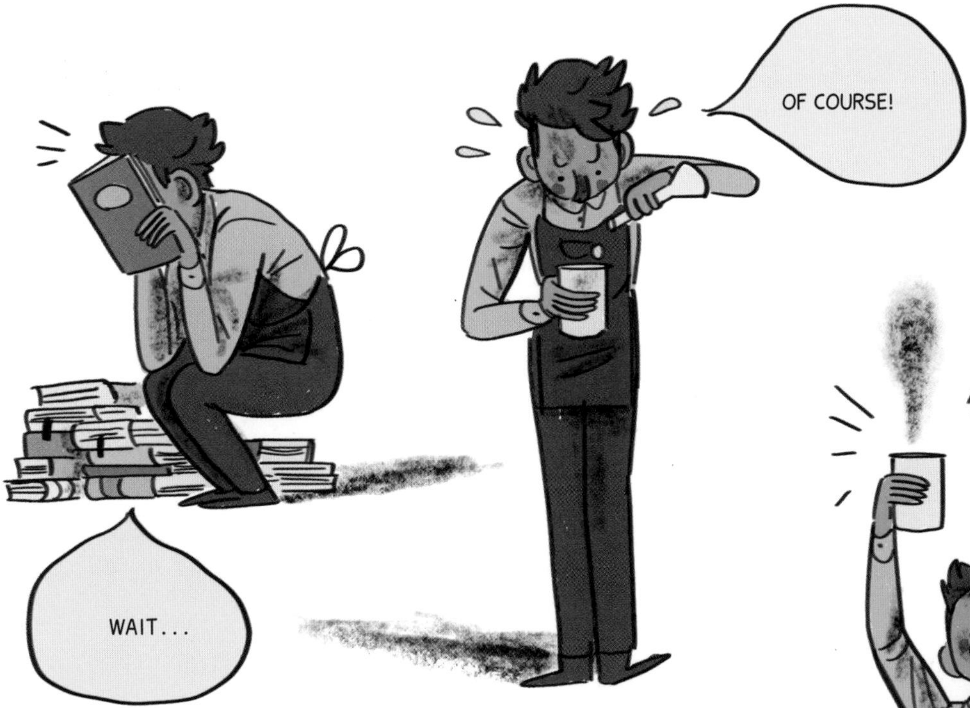
WAIT . . .
OF COURSE!

DON'T WORRY ABOUT MAKING A MISTAKE. TRY AGAIN, PERSIST. AFTER ALL, IF IT DOESN'T GO WELL THE FIRST TIME, WHO KNOWS ABOUT THE NEXT ONE!

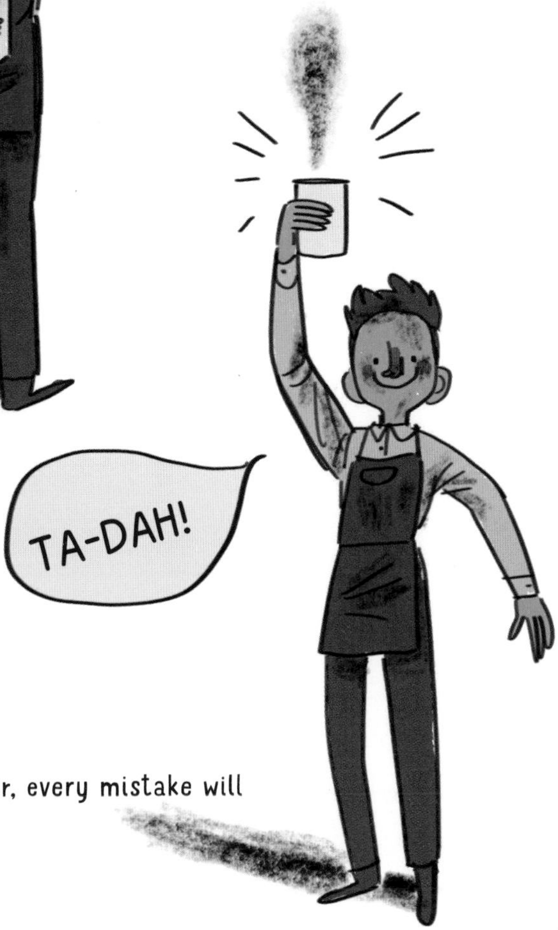
TA-DAH!

And even if you don't become an inventor, every mistake will bring you closer to something.

It's up to you to find out what it is!

MAX TEMPORELLI

is a physicist who has been involved in the dissemination of scientific, technological, and innovation culture for 25 years. He carries out these activities in university classrooms, on the internet, in museums, in publishing, on radio, and on television. Temporelli is the author of several books and has appeared on various TV programs on the subjects of science and technology. Since 2017, he has been the author and voice of a podcast on cultural geniuses and has been a featured TED Talks® speaker. In 2016, he was the recipient of the Federico Faggin Innovation Award.

BARBARA GOZZI

is senior editor and partner of the extremely skilled storytelling agency Book on a Tree.

AGNESE INNOCENTE

has worked as a sole author on comic book adaptations of great classics of children's literature. For years she has collaborated with various companies in the US, including Disney, as well as various Italian publishing houses. In 2021, she won the Andersen Prize for Best Comic Book.

When Everything Went Wrong © 2022 White Star s.r.l.
White Star Kids® is a registered trademark property of White Star s.r.l.
All rights reserved. Printed in China. No part of this book may be used or reproduced in any manner whatsoever without written permission except in the case of reprints in the context of reviews.

Andrews McMeel Publishing
a division of Andrews McMeel Universal
1130 Walnut Street, Kansas City, Missouri 64106

www.andrewsmcmeel.com

23 24 25 26 27 SDB 10 9 8 7 6 5 4 3 2 1

ISBN: 978-1-5248-8042-2

Library of Congress Control Number: 2022945731

Translated by Inga Sempel

Editor: Erinn Pascal
Art Director: Julie Barnes
Production Editor: Brianna Westervelt
Production Manager: Julie Skalla

Made by:
RR Donnelley (Guangdong) Printing Solutions Company Ltd
Address and location of manufacturer:
No. 2, Minzhu Road, Daning, Humen Town,
Dongguan City, Guangdong Province, China 523930
1st Printing – 12/5/22

ATTENTION: SCHOOLS AND BUSINESSES
Andrews McMeel books are available at quantity discounts with bulk purchase for educational, business, or sales promotional use. For information, please e-mail the Andrews McMeel Publishing Special Sales Department: sales@amuniversal.com.